Georgiana
Feminist Reformer of the West

COMO LA SOMBRA
HUYE LA HORA

"Sun-dial in Mr. K[irby]'s Garden, Santa Cruz," by Mary Hallock Foote, from "A Sea-Port on the Pacific," *Scribner's Monthly* 16 (August 1878), p. 458. "In 1874, the sundial belonging to [the mission] Santa Cruz stood in the garden of one D. Ricardo Kirby on Mission Street, Santa Cruz. Carved in the stone face are these words: 'Como la Sombra Huye la Hora' (Like a shadow the hour goes by)," from Edith Buckland Webb, *Indian Life at the Old Missions*. Reprint. (Lincoln: University of Nebraska Press, 1982) p. 37.

Georgiana
Feminist Reformer of the West

The Journal of Georgiana Bruce Kirby
1852–1860

With biography based on research of
Helen Giffen, Carolyn Swift, and Judith Steen
Edited by Carolyn Swift and Judith Steen

Foreword by Madeleine B. Stern

Santa Cruz County Historical Trust
Santa Cruz, California
1987

Published by Santa Cruz County Historical Trust
118 Cooper Street
Santa Cruz, California 95060

Designed by Charles Prentiss

Library of Congress Cataloging-in-Publication Data

Kirby, Georgiana Bruce, 1818–1887.
    Georgiana : feminist reformer of the West.
    Bibliography: p.
    Includes index.
    1. Kirby, Georgiana Bruce, 1818–1887--Diaries
2. Feminists--California--Santa Cruz--Diaries.
3. Frontier and pioneer life--California--Santa Cruz.
4. Santa Cruz (Calif.)--Biography. I. Giffen, Helen S.
(Helen Smith), 1893–   . II. Swift, Carolyn, 1948–
III. Steen, Judith, 1940–   . IV. Title.
HQ1413.K57A3 1987   305.4'2'0924   87-20463
ISBN 0–940283–02–6 (pbk.)

Support for this publication provided by
FRED D. MCPHERSON JR. PUBLICATION FUND
SANTA CRUZ COUNTY HISTORICAL TRUST

DEDICATION

to

Jeannette Rowland
Phyllis Patten
Margaret Koch

Three women who through their leadership in the
Santa Cruz Historical Society, their writing,
and their research have helped preserve
the history of Santa Cruz.

Contents

List of Illustrations

Foreword

After a lecture trip in the early 1870s, the Transcendental philosopher and educator Bronson Alcott, father of Louisa May, reported: "The West is shaping an Ideal Republic for us. . . . Here in New England we live more for the past, venture more cautiously into the future." If indeed the West shaped an "Ideal Republic" for the East, Georgiana Bruce Kirby played a part in that shaping. She brought to the West the intellectual insights considered by many "the exclusive privileges of the East." Her sights were almost always fixed upon the future. Hence the journal of her early years in Santa Cruz forms the record not only of one woman's adjustments and adaptations to a new land, but of the transitions and shaping of the land itself. As such, it is a document of extraordinary interest.

"Born of grief" in England in 1818, Georgiana eventually found work in Boston, Massachusetts. There, despite her humble beginnings, she was able to educate herself, appease her intellectual thirsts, and partake of the ferment of reform that agitated New England. In the East, Georgiana was exposed to the "newness" in its various anti-establishment forms: phrenology and spiritualism, dress reform and temperance, Transcendentalism, the rights of labor and the rights of women. She spent three years in the socialist community of Brook Farm, near West Roxbury, Massachusetts, where the like-minded basked in all phases of the "newness." She met Margaret Fuller, America's greatest feminist, soon to become a citizen of the world. Through Margaret she was introduced to the redoubtable Eliza Farnham, progressive and controversial matron of the women's prison at Sing Sing, New York, for whom Georgiana served as assistant during the 1840s. In that institution the reforms to which both women subscribed were applied to penology. As for the reform known as abolition, Georgiana's anti-slavery impulses were intensified when, teaching in the Midwest, she was requested to judge the color of her pupils' skin (and segregate them accordingly) by means of tinted cards.

Such was the intellectual background of the woman who in May 1850 started the long journey west for the purpose of sharing El Dorado with her former associate Eliza Farnham. Eliza, who had inherited El Rancho La Libertad from her husband, had invited Georgiana to that 200-acre farm in Santa Cruz. There these formidable and stalwart women practiced the dress reform they preached, donned Turkish pants or Albanian costume to ride across country, shared the problems of farming, and exchanged news and views of the books and reforms of the East.

On 23 March 1852, the combined household was broken up, for on that day both women were married, Eliza for the second time, Georgiana for the first. Georgiana Bruce, now Georgiana Bruce Kirby, moved with her husband Richard, a tanner, to the Rancho La Salud. She was on her way to becoming an "institution" in Santa Cruz, a woman who would serve tea to Mark Twain and ride over the mountain to visit with Horace Greeley, who would act as "a natural spearhead in many causes," and help shape the West into Bronson Alcott's "Ideal Republic."

It was not until 14 December 1852 that Georgiana began the journal that would reanimate the germinal years from 1852 to 1860, in the course of which she came to know Santa Cruz and Santa Cruz came to know her. Written purportedly for her unborn child, the entries merit a far more extended readership. Here she has encapsulated the place—the rancho "with its hollows and gulches and noble sweep of hills," its mines and farms, its weather, even the "starved existence" of its newspaper, the *Santa Cruz News*. She mentions the discovery of gold at Siant and in the Rincon, the price of staples, the cost of freight to San Francisco, the presence of maggots in the crops. The crops of course have a place in these pages: the planting of potatoes, the sowing of barley, the setting out of strawberry plants—along with the tending of chickens.

The external world of the rancho forms the backdrop for Georgiana's interior world. Despite the sympathetic relationship between husband and wife, exhaustion vies with pecuniary problems, and the birth and rearing of children leave her little leisure except for thinking. She sums up her labors, and we find summed up the labors of most pioneer women settlers: "to cook, wash, iron, houseclean, bake, mend, nurse, write letters, receive and pay visits, read, etc., all of which was necessary if I would really live like a civilized being, was too much for one person." Yet to those labors Georgiana adds the teaching of French and German, morals and manners to "irreverent" western children.

The people of Santa Cruz do not escape her sometimes scathing pen. "Keenly sensitive to the characters of those about" her, Georgiana did not suffer fools, or bores, or braggarts gladly. Of one she wrote: "By talking one-quarter as much he would have twenty times the influence." Another she castigates as "a shallow, conceited, dogmatic, insolent, pro-slavery braggart." Georgiana is indeed judgmental about members of neighboring families or visitors from the mission. "There is not one person of cultivated, enlarged mind in the place. Sometimes I seem quite collapsed for the want of spiritual food." Some are "real puritans" who "have the spirit that a century or so ago would have roasted people." It is the "ignorant, white people from the slave states" who "are the curse of California." "I should live," she ruminates, "where I can have the sympathy of abolitionists." She recognizes within herself the need for a "companion of her own sex" such as she has found in Eliza Farnham. "We are so suggestive to each other."

As Georgiana puts it, a "pleasant and healthy excitement" is produced by "the friction of mind on mind." That friction, that intellectual excitement, she seeks at all times. She finds it primarily in the books she reads. Through literature she attains the life of the intellect. Her books—Guizot's *Civilization of Modern Europe,* Thackeray's "aimless, superficial and unimproving" novels—have probably all been shipped by steamer from publishers in the East (perhaps from the phrenologist-publishers Fowler & Wells), rounded the Horn, and arrived at long last in San Francisco or in Santa Cruz. Through them Georgiana delves into "Channing's mild moralities, Carlyle's indignant ravings, Parker's bold analysis of . . . religious sentiments." She studies Browning's *Paracelsus* and compares his philosophy with that of the Swedenborgian Henry James, Sr. She devours *Uncle Tom*, finding in anti-slavery literature "the bread of life." As she observes: "Without this connecting link I could not live so far from any centre of thought. My mind would shrink to the modicum of those with whom I associate and growth be a mere word in the dictionary." And elsewhere she writes: "It is good to read just enough to stimulate thought."

Georgiana constantly seeks to stimulate her thoughts. Often she indulges in a kind of phrenological self-analysis, chiding herself for want of "self-esteem and concentrativeness," for allowing her nobler sentiments to lie dormant. "I am . . . one who loves to help develop character and intellect aright." And so, cooking and keeping house, farming and caring for her children, she snatches the moments for reading and for thinking. The doctrine she has carried from the East through her earlier exposure to the reforms of the day is crystallized. It develops, as the years pass, into a political philosophy that gleams through the pages of her journal.

Georgiana boasts the morality of the idealist, the politics of the reformer. She is adamantly hostile to the love of "material gain" and the lack of sentiment that seem to characterize mid-nineteenth-century America. With a perceptive eye she notes "the evils of a new country with no old institutions," and she pinpoints "the moving spirit" of California as "an external one," characterized by such traits as "generosity, cheerfulness, hope" but without a "love of abstract ideas." The sham and the false in morality and sentiment she shuns, along with the "irrational" church dogmas, "total depravity and eternal punishment." She views anti-slavery as "the great question of the day," as indeed it was. In an America "where it is the universal custom to call sin virtue—to boast of oppression and brag of . . . freedom . . . all in a breath—to hate with a wolfish hatred those who dare to advocate the most obvious right," Georgiana Bruce Kirby sees "nothing but approaching despotism."

In the life that was left to her after the close of her short journal she did what she could to ward off that "approaching despotism." She accomplished this not only by her writings (her recollections of Brook Farm, her autobiography, her study on motherhood) but by her active championship of great contemporary issues. When the anti-slavery cause gave way to the cause of women's rights, Georgiana enlisted in that crusade, not only as observer and recorder but as participant. Indeed, the final stunning sentences of her journal give promise of that feminist allegiance: "My thoughts in those days ran on the freedom of women—on what slaves we are and have been to the decisions of men. A hundred years hence it will be looked on with astonishment that a woman is prevented by public opinion from having a child unless she finds someone whom she wishes to accept as master for life."

At once iconoclast and builder, this dauntless woman from the East lent herself to the shaping of the West until it became an "Ideal Republic." In the book that follows, her life has been skillfully and painstakingly narrated through the combined efforts of Helen Giffen, Carolyn Swift, and Judith Steen, replete with the full panoply of extensive and informative notes, chronology, genealogy, and bibliography. The journal itself has been edited with scrupulous care and scholarship. Short in length but long in significance, it elucidates the life of the West at mid-century, and it brings to life the woman who lived it.

Madeleine B. Stern
New York

Preface

More than ten years ago, the Santa Cruz Historical Society considered publishing the journal of Georgiana Bruce Kirby. Several members had read a typed copy of the journal in Special Collections at the McHenry Library, University of California, Santa Cruz. Through member Barbara Giffen, the society met her cousin, author Helen Giffen. Since the 1930's, Helen had been researching Georgiana's life. She had written a lengthy biography based on her research and on Georgiana's autobiographical *Years of Experience*. Helen offered her manuscript to the society for publication. The society decided to publish an edited and annotated edition of the journal with an introductory biography that incorporated Helen's manuscript and research. Local writer and journalist Carolyn Swift, who was interested in Georgiana and Eliza Farnham, received a grant from the society to draft the biography, expanding on the latter part of Georgiana's life in Santa Cruz and her activities in women's rights and reform movements—areas which required additional investigation. With my experience as a reference librarian and my involvement in local history, I agreed to oversee the project, to provide research, bibliographic, and editorial assistance, and to edit and annotate the journal.

It has indeed been a lengthy project! Over the decade, the Santa Cruz Historical Society has merged with the Santa Cruz County Society for Historical Preservation and become the Santa

Cruz County Historical Trust. Fred D. McPherson, Jr., in a beneficent gesture to the community and to the vitalization of Santa Cruz County history, has endowed a publication fund. Dedicated individuals and organizations have produced significant resources, allowing identification and verification of many references in the journal. Especially helpful have been the recently published *Santa Cruz Daily Surf Local News Index, from the Beginning in 1883 through 1900* and the *Santa Cruz Sentinel Local News Index, from June 1856 through May 1884*, compiled, organized, and published by the Friends of the Santa Cruz Public Libraries. Also important for Santa Cruz County historical research is the *Indexed Cemetery Records of Santa Cruz County*, compiled and published by the Genealogical Society of Santa Cruz County. All three of these invaluable sources were produced under the leadership of Sara Bunnett. Donald Clark's monumental *Santa Cruz County Place Names*, which the Trust had the privilege to publish in 1986, has become a treasured, essential reference. The many biographical and historical works that have been published in the past few years on women in nineteenth-century America and the American West have provided ideas, inspiration, and encouragement.

Because the project spanned so many years, several individuals read various drafts and offered sound advice. These comments helped us focus on what we wanted to accomplish in a relatively brief book. Our goal was to present the journal of an educated, outspoken woman who brought her reformist ideas and ideals from the East and transplanted them into the fertile but isolated pioneer environment of the mid-nineteenth-century American West. In addition to placing her life within the broader historical context of national women's rights activities and other social, political, and intellectual movements of the period, we also wanted to identify local events and individuals that influenced her life and linked the two coasts. One of the strongest and most enduring of these ties was that of her friendship with Eliza Farnham.

Some who read early drafts commented that there was too much emphasis on Eliza Farnham, and that this was, after all, a biography of Georgiana. We cut ruthlessly. But it is indeed difficult to throw a shade over the brilliant blaze of Eliza, who was twenty-eight years old when she met twenty-five-year-old Georgiana. For the next twenty years, the influence of one woman on the other was both intimate and profound. The support that Georgiana received from Eliza was life-sustaining. When Eliza left Georgiana alone in California—alone, that is, with a husband and two children—Georgiana's plaintive cry in her journal was, without her "How can I live?"

Georgiana's indefatigable self-reliance, courage, and personal conviction, however, far outshone her dependence on Eliza. The biography emphasizes the intellectual side of Georgiana rather than the human. The journal frequently portrays a shrewish, impatient, overly critical personality. In fairness, one cannot judge too harshly private writings that candidly describe the frustrations and the feelings of isolation of an outspoken woman. But there is also a gentle side of Georgiana, for she was, indeed, a generous, kind-hearted woman with a love of nature, flowers, and gardening, one who decried her perceived deficiencies in imagination, taste, and delicacy, but who also expressed cosmopolitan interests in music, art, architecture, fashion—one who always stopped to view a patch of yellow flowers in a green field. She had a romantic side that might have been expressed by describing the carefree camping trip she took up the coast with her soon-to-be-husband Richard Kirby, Eliza, and another male friend; it was a lighthearted expedition to pick wild strawberries and cook beef over a campfire. She was sometimes insecure and self-consciously introspective; she had an incisive mind and was an articulate and passionate speaker and writer.

Georgiana was truly as much an adventurer as the more flamboyant and eccentric Eliza. She was always eager to seek new frontiers. As she phrased it in her autobiography, "But as for me I could never cry at parting." Whether leaving her family in England and journeying to France or Canada or the United States; or, setting out on her own with little money and no job and seeking employment as a single woman in Illinois or Missouri or ultimately in the little community of Santa Cruz, California—she ventured and persevered. After leaving behind friends on the East Coast who were the leading thinkers and writers of nineteenth-century America, she could still comment optimistically in the autobiography published shortly before her death, "I can honestly say that my best days came after I was fifty, and that at sixty-six I am happier than I was at eighteen." She was happy at sixty-six living in unsophisticated Santa Cruz without intellectual stimulation or her dearest friend Eliza and with the recent loss of two of her beloved children and the constant pain from arthritis— now that is a remarkable woman!

While some felt that too much attention is devoted to Eliza, others felt that Richard Kirby, Georgiana's husband, is not given the attention he deserves. Much more might have been written about Richard and his relationship with Georgiana. His kind, generous, patient, courageous, and industrious nature often shines through the entries in her journal. His love of Georgiana and his support of her and her often very unpopular causes earned him Georgiana's highest compliment of "devoted friend."

Since many copies of the diary have been made, some probably being copies of copies, the text chosen to edit is that made by Helen Giffen. Comparisons were made with the transcript in the UCSC Library and with that published in the 1930's in the *Santa Cruz News* by Leon Rowland. Obvious typographical errors were corrected. Paragraphing was sometimes added for clarity, as was punctuation. Names in the journal were often spelled differently in each typed version, though overall the differences between the various typescripts were minor.

The location of the original journal is unknown. Helen Giffen copied the journal in 1933 when it was in the possession of Bruce Chalmers, Georgiana's great grandson and sole surviving descendant. Mr. Chalmers has led the life of a soldier of fortune and, in the spirit of his great grandmother Georgiana, has had adventurous experiences in many countries. Charles McCabe, the late *San Francisco Chronicle* columnist, featured Chalmers in columns during the early 1970's, when he was the owner of a bar in the Alhambra in Spain. He no longer owns the bar and several years ago was reported to have moved to the interior of Spain. The mystery of his whereabouts adds a final colorful chapter to this unconventional family's history.

Georgiana titled her journal, "Das Tagebuch," German for "the daybook." She began the journal a week after her thirty-fourth birthday, when she had been in California almost two-and-one-half years and had been married to Richard Kirby for nine months. In fifty-one entries, dated from December 14, 1852, to January 26, 1860, some as short as one line and sometimes with lapses of as much as sixteen months, she recorded her thoughts and observations, mentioning names from her past, her correspondents, the books and newspapers she loved to read, and her friends and critics in Santa Cruz.

In identifying names within the journal, I was confronted with the problem with which anyone involved in nineteenth-century history must contend—women are lost. The old county histories chronicle very few women, and those that are included often are not given an entry in the index. Maiden names are buried, literally; one often finds that cemetery records, death records, or obituaries provide the only clues. I spent more time perusing the center column of indexes than I did the alphabetical surname entries. Unfortunately, there are several women in this text who go unidentified, or who appear as mere appendages to entries for their husbands. This is regrettable, for many fascinating women are hidden under references to "Mrs. This" or "Mrs. That."

I hope that the journal, the biography, and the names of the women pioneers scattered throughout the text and included in the footnotes will intrigue others. Perhaps future writers will devote many more pages to Georgiana, Eliza, and those women of California who not only gave birth, reared families, and managed homes, but also played significant roles in educational, social, and political reform movements.

Judith Steen
September, 1987

Acknowledgements

During the course of the project, we have received assitance from many sources that we gratefully acknowledge. The Santa Cruz Historical Trust thanks Helen Giffen for the generous contribution of her manuscript, her continuing gracious advice, and her efforts to preserve Georgiana's work. The Trust thanks also Thomas McCarthy for his legal expertise; Hal Morris for his business recommendations; Charles Prentiss for his graphics talent; and Frank Perry for his publishing advice. Helen acknowledges Barbara Giffen for her time, patience, and assistance; Bruce Chalmers, Georgiana's great-grandson; the late Leon and Jeannette Rowland for their advice and encouragement; the late Mrs. Amy Goodwin Harvey and Mrs. Walter Byrne for their personal recollections of Georgiana; and the late Thomas McHugh for his insights. We thank all those libraries and archives and their devoted staff who collect, make accessible, and provide reference to the past, especially, the McHenry Library of the University of California, Santa Cruz, the Santa Cruz Public Library, the California Historical Society Library, the California State Library, the Huntington Library, and the California Society of Pioneers Library. Carolyn Swift and I wish to thank Sandy Lydon for reading drafts of the work and offering critical comments and for his unending, enthusiastic support; Madeleine B. Stern for her beautifully written introduction; Fred D. McPherson, Jr., whose generous financial support enabled the Trust to establish The Fred D. McPherson Jr. Publication Fund which allows publication of this book; Alan Ritch and Rosemary Brogan for their valuable comments on final drafts; the Trust's Publications Committee—Joyce Miller, Jill Perry, Alverda Orlando, and especially the Chair, Stan Stevens, for reading the manuscript, identifying elusive errors, offering sound advice and valuable assistance, and generally keeping the project moving; Donald Clark, for his always generous and cheerful advice and for the high standards that we endeavored to reach; Sara Bunnett and her tireless corps of volunteer indexers; and Joe Michalak for his generous contribution of time and energy in keying the manuscript on his computer, making corrections, offering suggestions, and maintaining his irrepressible sense of humor and unqualified loyalty and support of the project; and to all our faithful, long-suffering friends who thought that we would never finish.

Judith Steen
September, 1987

Georgiana Bruce Kirby: A Chronology
with
Significant Dates in Women's and American History

1818   Georgiana Bruce (GBK) born Bristol, England, December 7.

1821   Emma Willard founds female seminary at Troy, N.Y., the first to provide secondary education for women.

1823   **GBK's mother remarries.**
GBK attends boarding school at Enfield, near London.
Family moves to Camden Town, London.

1828   **Family moves to Margate.**
First strike of women workers over wages takes place in Dover, New Hampshire.
GBK attends school for young ladies.

1832   **GBK confirmed in the Episcopal Church.**

1833   **GBK teaches stepbrothers and Spencer children.**
Oberlin College (Ohio) becomes first institution of higher education to admit women; first graduate 1837.

1834   **GBK in Paris with Spencer family.**

1835   **GBK returns with Spencers to England.**
GBK leaves for Canada with Spencer family.

1837   **GBK leaves Canada and returns to England.**
First national Anti-Slavery Convention of American Women meets in New York.
Mary Lyon founds Mt. Holyoke Seminary (later College), in Massachusetts, first women's college offering education comparable to men's colleges.

1838   **GBK at Gannetts in Boston.**

1841   **GBK at Brook Farm, September.**

1844   **GBK leaves Brook Farm, April. Appointed assistant to Eliza Farnham (EF) at Sing Sing Prison.**

1845   **GBK leaves Sing Sing; travels to St. Louis; begins teaching at Monticello Academy in Illinois.**
        Margaret Fuller's *Woman in the Nineteenth Century* published, an early and influential work urging women's rights.

1846   **GBK teaches at Bonne Femme Plantation in Missouri.**
        GBK at Byberry and Westchester, Pennsylvania.
        Bear Flag Revolt.

1848   James Marshall discovers gold at Coloma, California.
        Treaty of Guadalupe Hildalgo cedes California to U.S.
        The first Women's Rights Convention held at Seneca Falls, New York, led by Lucretia Mott and Elizabeth Cady Stanton.

1849   **EF issues brideship circular, February; leaves for California, April.**
        Gold Rush.

1850   **EF arrives in Santa Cruz, February 22, at La Libertad, after two months in San Francisco.**
        GBK leaves for California, May; arrives in Santa Cruz October 18.
        Richard Kirby (RK) establishes tannery at Squabble Hollow (Glen Canyon).
        GBK and EF open school for girls in Santa Cruz, November.
        California admitted to the Union.

1850–   National Women's Rights Conference held annually.
1860

1851   **GBK works for Bryant Hill for six months in Pajaro.**
        Sojourner Truth, ex-slave, delivers in Akron, Ohio, her

famous speech.

1852   EF marries William Fitzpatrick, March 23.
GBK marries Richard Kirby, March 23; moves to Rancho La Salud.
Records first entry in Journal, December 14.

1853   At age 34, GBK gives birth to her first child, Ora Bruce, June 29.

1854   Kirbys move to Santa Cruz, near Mission, December.
First American day nursery opened in New York City for children of poor working mothers.

1855   RK moves to new tan yard, January. GBK's second child, Georgiana Bruce (Georgie), born, December 12.

1856   EF's *California Indoors and Out*, published; EF divorces Fitzpatrick and returns to New York.

1857   GBK's third child, Cornelia Maude, born, December 29.

1858   EF speaks at Women's Rights Convention in New York, May.

1859   EF returns to California.

1860   GBK records last entry in Journal, January 26.
Elizabeth Peabody organizes in Boston the first formal kindergarten in the United States.

1861   GBK's fourth child, Richard Bruce, born, April 16.
EF appointed matron at female department at Stockton (California) Insane Asylum; returns to New York in 1862; Volunteers as nurse at Gettysburg, 1863.

1861–   American Civil War.
1865

1863 RK sells tan yard and purchases property for new operation on Laurel Street.

1864 EF dies at age 49, New York City, December 15, buried in Friends Cemetery, Milton-on-Hudson, New York; *Woman and Her Era* published.

1865 GBK's fifth child, Phillip Bruce, born, January 2.

1869 GBK founds first local society of suffragists.
Wyoming Territory grants women suffrage.
National Woman Suffrage Association formed, led by Elizabeth Cady Stanton and Susan B. Anthony. American Woman Suffrage Association formed, led by Lucy Stone and Julia Ward Howe.
Transcontinental railroad completed.

1870 Petition to California State Legislature for women's suffrage amendment.

1870– GBK publishes articles in *Old and New, Overland*
1872 *Monthly,* and *Santa Cruz Sentinel.*

1871 Susan B. Anthony and Elizabeth Cady Stanton in Santa Cruz, August.

1874 Women's Christian Temperance Union formed by Frances Willard.

1877 Mary Hallock Foote visits GBK.
GBK's *Transmission* published.

1879 GBK's daughter Georgiana dies, at age 23, November 11.

1884 GBK's son Phillip dies, at age 19, October 13.

1887 GBK's *Years of Experience* published.
GBK dies at age 68 in Santa Cruz, January 27.

1892   GBK's son Richard dies, at age 31, December 14.

1895   GBK's daughter Ora dies, at age 42, November 2.

1897   GBK's only son-in-law, Charles E. Brown, dies at age 41, November 23.

1904   RK dies, at age 86, July 14.

1911   California grants women suffrage.

1913   Margaret Bruce Brown Chalmers, GBK's only grandchild, dies at age 26, January 24.

1920   Ratification of the Nineteenth Amendment.

1925   GBK's last surviving child, Cornelia Maude Kirby Brown, dies at age 67, June 2.

The Life of
Georgiana Bruce Kirby

I. Years of Experience, 1818–1850

Georgiana Bruce Kirby was born in Bristol, England, on December 7, 1818, to Susan Stradwick Bruce and the deceased Captain Francis Bruce. "Born of grief" is the phrase she later used to describe her birth and the family misfortune that had occurred a few months before.[1]

> My father, who died at sea three months previous to this event, was a Scotchman from Argyleshire. His life, from the time of early boyhood, had, however, been passed on the ocean. At the time he met my mother he was sailing as captain of one of his own merchantmen. He was a man of more character than cultivation, entertaining what would, even now, be considered radical views; just and honorable, kindhearted and straightforward. My mother, a highly educated woman for that day, was the daughter of Edmund Stradwick, Esq., whose private history formed a romance that fed my childish imagination. Her union with my father was considered somewhat of a mésalliance. It was of short duration, however, for when his first child, my sister C[aroline], was less than two years old, my father died at sea of a fever.[2]

Georgiana's English girlhood lacked much of the security, warmth, and education she craved. Her only years of contentment were the very early ones. At the age of three, she was sent to the village school with her sister. Georgiana was an "unchildlike child," curious and observant, who desired "forbidden knowledge" and immediately began to question the "devine arrangement of things, as set forth in the church catechism."[3] When Georgiana was in her fifth year, her mother remarried and the family moved to a large country estate with spacious gardens midst peaceful surroundings. This halcyon existence was short-lived, however. The unfortunate second marriage, to a man named Thomas Bellamy, was the source of a series of hardships that soon ended Georgiana's carefree childhood. Bellamy's investment of the family's inheritance proved foolhardy, and two more children were born into a household that was fast becoming insolvent. Georgiana was taken from the boarding school that she had attended for one year at Enfield, near London, and trained as the family maid. Except for the learning she achieved on her own, her schooling ceased for nearly six years.

The Bellamys' declining finances forced them to leave the country mansion for a modest house in Camden Town, London. The next move was to the coastal town of Margate, where Georgiana was kept so occupied with housework that she sometimes hid in a closet under the garret stairs to steal brief minutes with the family's few remaining books, including her favorites, *Robinson Crusoe* and the *Refutation of Paine's Age of Reason*, which convinced her that Paine was right in his attack on religious organization.

"I remember little besides disorder and discomfort at the home in M[argate]," she said. "I was now ten years old, and whatever disagreeable work was within the compass of a child's strength fell to my share."[4] Eventually she was permitted to attend a school for young ladies at Margate, but for only one year. Here she was taught a bit of arithmetic, geography, and French, some grammar, a smattering of English poets, and the rudiments of music.

Georgiana entered her adolescence filled with questions— questions not only about her prospective future as a governess, but also about traditional moral attitudes, societal values, and religious doctrines. The basis for her belief in the ideals of religious liberalism began to develop. She later observed:

> A realizing sense of your own unworthiness was the pre-

requisite to a religious life. You were the child of the Devil, who was the father of lies....Now I did not feel that I was *very* bad. I was conscious of no burden. I knew that I had performed hundreds of disagreeable duties cheerfully from the sentiment of obedience and love, and to invalidate my motives thus was an outrage on truth and justice.[5]

"How much I wished that the Almighty had been a mother, an infinite mother! *She* would never have planned an endless hell," Georgiana reasoned.[6]

Regardless of her private views, Georgiana was confirmed as an Episcopalian shortly before her fourteenth birthday. Soon afterward, she began teaching. Her first pupils were her stepbrothers and the three children of Mr. and Mrs. Charles Spencer, summer visitors to Margate.[7] The Spencers were pleased with Georgiana, and when they left for France, where Spencer was to work as a court reporter for an English newspaper, they offered her a position as governess. It was an opportunity that she eagerly accepted.

"I was just turned of fifteen when I stood for the last time on the sands at M[argate] in company with the S[pencer]s and all our household, waiting to catch sight of the smoke of the Calais steamer," she recalled. "The boys and my mother were crying, and it seemed as if I were a being devoid of natural affection, because I had no tears to mingle with theirs."[8]

The Spencers' stay in France was brief, as their younger daughter died shortly after they arrived. Georgiana returned with them to London, satisfied with her role as "elder daughter" with entrée to the city's cultural life. "Modern literature was being rapidly created at that time. [Sir Walter] Scott was publishing his last novel.... The warfare over Byron, his poems and conduct, still raged fiercely.... Napoleon had been dead just long enough to ensure a large crop of 'memoirs,' 'souvenirs,' and histories." And Georgiana read them all.[9]

The family had been in London for only a year-and-a-half when Spencer decided to emigrate to Canada. The young governess was asked to accompany them; once again, she readily accepted.

Spencer chose a homesite at Melbourne in the Province of

Quebec, close to the American border. Many of the inhabitants of this French-Canadian settlement were New Englanders who had crossed the border to take advantage of Canada's liberal land laws and who brought with them their American customs, religious beliefs, and democratic tendencies. They observed Thanksgiving, questioned orthodoxy, and treated one another, male and female, more as equals.

Georgiana joined Spencer as a teacher at the village school and began seriously to consider a career in teaching.   More importantly, she was captivated by the ideas introduced to her in these new surroundings. She re-examined her views on religion when she became acquainted with the Universalist sect, whose tenets affirmed universal salvation and denied belief in hell. She identified with the more liberated social structure, the greater freedom of intellectual expression, and the independence of pioneer life.

She particularly admired the women who courageously adopted untraditional roles and boldly accepted the challenges of new frontiers. Georgiana learned to spin wool, make candles, bake bread, and milk a cow. Her best friend was a Methodist woman of forty-three, though Georgiana was only seventeen.

After two-and-one-half years in Canada, the Spencer family decided to return to England; Georgiana, though she would have preferred to remain, dutifully accompanied them home. But English life no longer suited her, and in a short time, she again crossed the Atlantic. On this voyage she was alone with very little money, traveling with the hope that she might find a job as a governess or nurse. She was in luck; on board she was introduced to the Reverend Ezra Stiles Gannett, who was returning from Europe with his wife and child.

The Reverend Mr. Gannett was a distinguished Unitarian minister, the pastor of Boston's Federal Street Church. A graduate of Harvard, he was secretary, and later, president, of the American Unitarian Association.

After meeting the minister's wife, Georgiana was given the job of nursemaid at a wage of one dollar a week. Even though she had not intended to work in such a menial capacity, she accepted the offer. This decision, however, presented her with a problem. She had come to the United States seeking greater independence and opportunity, yet she had taken a position beneath her class. She discovered that her sought-after liberation was severely compromised, for the New England emphasis on class distinction was in many ways stricter than that of her homeland.

"It did not take long for me to learn that the caste spirit in Boston was harder, more insensitive than in the mother-country," she said. "Its basis was not inherited estates and titles, but descent either from those Puritans who came over in the Mayflower, or from other early emigrants of that class."[10]

Both physically and emotionally, life was difficult as a nursemaid for the Gannetts. Georgiana was obliged to make many adjustments—learning to curb her tongue, to repress her unasked for opinions, and to refrain from familiar advances. She resented the "frigid exclusiveness" of the women. "I had far more quiet self-esteem than the lady members of the family, who seemed constantly on the alert lest I should be moved to cross the line of demarkation," she wrote. "Sometimes I inwardly resented the petty assumptions of those only a few years older than myself and with less intelligence."[11]

She found the Reverend Mr. Gannett benevolent and sympathetic, but his wife was stiff and uncompromising. It was only the visits of Gannett's niece, a fourteen-year-old named Deborah, known as "Ora," that provided Georgiana any pleasant companionship. "Why don't you get away from this nunnery?" Ora asked Georgiana. "I would go west and teach school, if I were you."[12]

For more than three years she endured "the furnace of Boston conservatism," cut off from the social amenities of the cultivated and refined, lacking any chance to break the dullness of daily routines with intellectual debates. She was lonely, and when the Reverend Mr. Gannett suggested she send for one of her step-brothers, she seized the opportunity and asked fourteen-year-old Edmund Bellamy to join her.

Although Georgiana had long ago saved the money she needed to leave the Gannetts' home, she stayed in part because of the books in the family library and the intellectual excitement of the literary world of Boston. "This literature was just what I wanted....I believe I devoured every thing written by the cultivated Unitarian clergy of the United Kingdom as well as the

United States, while confined to this well-warmed apartment,"
she said. The study of Unitarianism finally disposed for Georgiana
"the Devil, the Trinity, innate depravity, blood-atonement, and
hell."[13]

During this period, Boston was "the cradle of modern ideas
for the continent, to live there...was to receive the full force of the
electric current," Georgiana later recalled.[14]

> In this modern Athens, or in the small towns grouped
> around it, between the years 1802 and 1811, were born
> those men whom nature destined to take the leading part
> in that revolution of thought which distinguished the
> era. Consequently, in 1840 most of them were in their
> prime.... [William Ellery] Channing, the fervent, poetic,
> and powerful advocate of man's innate capacity for the
> good and beautiful, had nearly finished his labors....
> [William Lloyd] Garrison had brought many a broadside
> to bear on the national sin, and besides had challenged
> the world on the subject position of women.... [John
> Greenleaf] Whittier's martial strain and pathetic
> ballads were putting the mildly-named 'Conservatives'
> to open shame. [James Russell] Lowell, younger child of
> the muses, was modestly questioning his heritage of the
> divine afflatus. [Nathaniel] Hawthorne, [John Lothrop]
> Motley, [William Hickling] Prescott, stars of the first
> magnitude, were well above the horizon. [Ralph Waldo]
> Emerson was brooding a fresh series of spiritual
> aphorisms. Theodore Parker had just flung a bombshell
> into the respectable Unitarian camp; and lest genius
> should soar too far beyond human ken, the phrenologists
> had taken the platform, skull in hand, prepared to prove
> by it, or any other cranium in the audience, that each
> faculty of the mind occupied a definite location in the
> brain, and that, given the temperament, size was the
> measure of power.... Finally, George Ripley had
> assembled the advocates of the dignity and rights of
> labor, and organized the Brook Farm Association at West
> Roxbury.[15]

The Reverend Mr. Gannett increasingly realized his
servant's talent and intellect, but the prevailing caste of values

prevented him from providing her with any direct help. He did, however, find a solution; Georgiana and her brother were supplied with an introduction to the Reverend Mr. Ripley, founder of the human experiment at Brook Farm.

Situated on the fringe of West Roxbury, nine miles from Boston, Brook Farm was neither a socialistic nor a religious haven. It was instead an association devoted to education and agriculture, intended for men and women who wished to live in an environment of spiritual growth and mental stimulus.

The very idea of such an atmosphere was intensely appealing to Georgiana. She arrived at the Transcendentalist community in late September, 1841, and was greeted by Ora, the Gannetts' niece. At dinner that day, she was given the seat of honor next to Ripley and there met his niece, Sarah Stearns, an ardent abolitionist. On her right was Duncan Wells, who was preparing for college under the tutelage of Charles Dana. These people were the first among many who were to influence Georgiana during those early days at Brook Farm and who were to become lifelong friends.

She soon considered the time at Brook Farm as the happiest thus far in her life. The days were divided into periods for study, chores, letter-writing, walks, meetings, and intellectual discourse. One of her best friends was Abby Morton, who would later become the noted author Abby Morton Diaz. In the company of proven talent and budding greatness, she felt accepted for her own worth and discovered that her mind was quick enough to keep pace with her contemporaries.

Shortly after Georgiana came to Brook Farm, she met Margaret Fuller, the editor of the Transcendentalist journal *The Dial*, who was a supporter of the Farm society, although she took no active part in its affairs. Fuller arrived for dinner one evening and was seated next to Ripley. Georgiana stared with admiration, but felt an uncharacteristic shyness at the meeting. Fuller mistook this reticence for rudeness. Afterwards, Fuller wrote in her journal: "I felt the want of conventional refinement in the impudence with which one of the girls treated me."[16]

Seeing one another again on a walk the next day, the two women made amends. Thereafter, Georgiana considered it her privilege to give up her room for the author whenever she came to visit. During their private talks, she was given a glimpse of the life Fuller led in New York, where she wrote for Horace Greeley's *New York Tribune* and lived with his family on Turtle Bay.

Georgiana enjoyed a stimulating association with Brook Farm for three years. She studied music with John Sullivan Dwight and read German with Charles Dana. She met Elizabeth Peabody, in whose Boston bookshop Fuller delivered her famous "conversations," and the other Peabody sisters and their future husbands, Sophia and Nathaniel Hawthorne and Mary and Horace Mann. These were days of work, congenial companionship, and simple pleasures. Ralph Waldo Emerson spent a week, and Frances Ostinelli (later known as concert singer Signora Elisa Biscaccianti) stayed for a month. Charles Lane of England was, for Georgiana, among the more influential visiting scholars; he was an exponent of the idea of the power of the mother over the mind of the unborn child.[17]

Unfortunately, the Brook Farm society's main problem was money. One financial crisis was followed by another until the community subsisted chiefly upon what it could produce in tangible products such as eggs, milk, and potatoes.

During this struggle for solvency, Ripley grew interested in the works of Charles Fourier, a French socialist who proposed to divide society into "phalanxes," each with its own special interest. Several of Brook Farm's members encouraged Ripley to investigate this plan and to turn his organization from Transcendentalism to Fourierism.

Georgiana resisted the changes and resented the infiltration by adherents of Fourier. "The reputation of Brook Farm for brilliancy, wit, and harmless eccentricity was seriously compromised. The joyous spirit of youth was sobered. The outside community henceforth regarded the enterprise as a mechanical attempt to reform society, rather than a poetic attempt to regenerate it."[18]

Deciding to disassociate herself from the confusion, Georgiana, now twenty-five, left Brook Farm in April, 1844, and returned to Boston. She took refuge with the mother of Isaac Hecker, a member of Brook Farm, while her brother Edmund stayed on with the community.[19] Edmund was in poor health and a continual source of worry.

Seeking new direction, Georgiana asked the advice of Margaret Fuller, who suggested a meeting with the recently appointed matron of the Female State Prison at Sing Sing, New York. Georgiana traveled to the home of Horace Greeley to meet Eliza Farnham.

"Mrs. F. was said to be a woman of remarkable intellectual powers, with great firmness and courage, qualities which were necessary in dealing with criminals," said Georgiana. "She was now looking for suitable assistants, who would enter into her plans and be able to carry them out."[20]

Eliza's background paralleled Georgiana's in several ways. Born Eliza Wood Burhans in Rensselaerville, New York, on November 17, 1815, she had lost her mother at a young age and had been separated from the rest of her family. She was reared in rural New York by an aunt and uncle who treated her with indifference. Denied a formal education, Eliza was mostly self-taught until after her father died. At that time, another uncle agreed to sponsor her attendance at a seminary for young ladies at Albany.

When she was twenty, Eliza moved to Illinois, where she met and married Thomas Farnham. As an attorney, he supported his wife's literary talent and was a writer himself. But Farnham was also a wanderer, fascinated by the frontiers of California, and he left his family for long periods while he travelled in the western territory. Eliza was twenty-eight years old, alone, and the mother of two young sons, when she was appointed in 1844 to take charge of the women prisoners at Sing Sing.[21]

Fuller and Greeley planned the meeting between Eliza and Georgiana with the expectation that it would lead to Georgiana's employment. The prison matron wanted an associate who shared her ideas and who would work with her toward a reorganization of the women's facilities. The prison had been built several years before, after passage of a state bill that called for "a healthy location in the vicinity of some benevolent village whose inhabitants would feel an interest in the mental and moral improvement of these degraded beings."[22] However, the institution failed to meet the original standards. In fact, the prison board was assaulted by the inmates on an inspection tour. The administration was under fire and considerable opposition had sprung up regarding Mrs. Farnham's appointment. One board member, for example, had suggested that someone else be selected who did not make such a "display of feminine power."[23] In response, one of Eliza's supporters had replied: "We did not hire her to marry you. We brought her here to manage this prison."[24]

Georgiana's ideals and determination earned her appointment as one of four assistants. At the prison began a lifelong friendship between the two women—a friendship that changed the destiny of both of their lives.

Although she was intrigued by the humanistic methods employed by Mrs. Farnham, the new assistant matron was ill-prepared for the realities of prison life. She was shocked by such inmates as the murderess "Kane," whose face, Georgiana said, "was enough to terrify an unarmed man," or "Annie," whose cries for vinegar echoed throughout the cell-block.

"One of my first duties had been to examine the prison library...." she said. "This whole collection consisted of seventy-five copies of Baxter's 'Call to the Unconverted Sinner'; not another volume of any kind."[25]

In the environment where there had previously been rioting, Eliza and her staff promoted order and rehabilitation, introducing a more benevolent system of discipline and an instructional routine. Their efforts were eventually praised in the *History of Woman Suffrage*, edited by Elizabeth Cady Stanton, Susan B. Anthony, and Matilda Joslyn Gage:

> Eliza Farnham was in many respects a remarkable woman. As matron of the Sing Sing prison at one time, she introduced many humane improvements in the occupation and discipline of the women under her charge. She had a piano in the corridor, and with sweet music touched the tender chords in their souls. Instead of tracts on hell-fire and an angry God, she read aloud to them from Dickens' most touching stories. In every way, assisted by Mariana Johnson and Georgiana Bruce, she treated them as women, and not as criminals.[26]

Eliza based many of her methods upon the popular concepts of phrenology, in which she and Georgiana firmly believed. In 1846, Eliza published *Rationale of Crime, and Its Appropriate Treatment*, an American edition of a treatise by English phrenologist Marmaduke Blake Sampson.[27]

Years later, Georgiana wrote an analysis of her experiences during the one year of her employment with Eliza at the prison. "My passion for sympathizing, for putting myself in another's place, and, where necessary, advising, warning, comforting, and, as far as might be, taking the burden on myself, had had free play at Sing Sing." [28]

On her days off, Georgiana fled the prison to attend concerts and lectures with Margaret Fuller in New York. But the strain was too great; when her contract was up, the assistant resigned.

Her brother was now a printer's apprentice in Cincinnati, and Georgiana was eager to join him. Once more, Greeley came to her aid with an introduction to Moses Atwood, who lived in Alton, Illinois, a town located on a bluff overlooking the Mississippi River, twenty-three miles from St. Louis. He was certain that Atwood's influence could help her find a teaching job nearby.

She began her trip from New York to St. Louis in 1845 and arrived in Cincinnati without incident. Her brother met her at the docks and the two prepared to continue the journey together. But during the first night, a thief broke into their room and stole Georgiana's valuables, including Edmund's fare to St. Louis. She had little alternative except to leave him behind until other arrangements were made.

Two weeks after she left Cincinnati, Georgiana set foot on Missouri soil and was greeted with news of her brother's serious illness. Soon after, Edmund died. Fuller drew on her own finances to help Georgiana, who overcame her grief with the support of loyal friends.

Once she began to feel comfortable in her new surroundings, Georgiana enjoyed the freedom of space, the productivity and temperament of the West, as Illinois was then considered. She became fond of the people "who had forgotten the cramped life of the East, but had not divested themselves of the neatness and good taste...."[29] She lived in Alton, Illinois, at the home of Atwood, who was president of the Illinois Mutual Fire Insurance Company and a man considered to have broad vision and progressive ideas. While living in this household, Georgiana listened to lectures on "Magnetism" and met Emma Smith, widow of the Mormon prophet,

Joseph Smith. This was her first acquaintance with the Mormon religion and she was intrigued.

Atwood was not an avowed abolitionist, but he was a sympathizer and he sometimes hid escaped slaves in his woodshed. His guest, who had previously studied slavery in the abstract, was now keenly aware that only a river separated her from the nearest slave state. Georgiana saw first hand what she had read about in abolitionist literature and heard of at the anti-slavery meetings at Boston's Faneuil Hall.

She had no desire to teach where slavery existed and was happy when Atwood found her a temporary job as a music teacher at Monticello Seminary, at Godfrey's Prairie, a few miles from Alton; it was the first institution west of Philadelphia to be devoted entirely to the education of women. When the regular professor returned in the fall, Georgiana was offered another teaching job, but this one was in Missouri. She accepted with great reluctance.

She had misgivings from the moment she arrived at Providence and saw that no one had been sent to meet her for the ride to the "Bonne Femme" plantation owned by her new employer, David Hickman. Arrangements were made instead for her to stay in the home of a neighbor, who gave her a room that smelled strongly of lye soap, where light filtered through a filthy window, and the bed was made of corn husks. Beetles came from all corners, conspired to keep her awake, and crawled into her clothes. Thick mold grew on anything left out for more than twenty-four hours. Georgiana's request for better accommodations did result in a room with a fireplace, but the clapboards had pulled away from the chimney, allowing air to circulate freely. Rats replaced the beetles. Water was carried from a nearby field that had a spring, but there was no sanitary protection against drainage, and the family faced the risk of typhoid with every draught. Corn bread, hog meat, and coffee were the dietary staples.

The new teacher was disheartened. When rumors spread that she aided runaway slaves, Georgiana nearly lost her job; only the support of Captain Hickman saved it. He spoke in Georgiana's behalf and seemed to have a somewhat open mind on the subject of slavery. The captain listened to Georgiana's arguments for abolition with courtesy and tolerant amusement.

Increasingly, Georgiana grew more concerned for the slaves in the community. They sensed her sympathies and began to confide in her. This trust intensified her abolitionist beliefs.

In the beginning of her tenure, the teacher found the school was better than she had expected it to be. Here were pupils both diligent and docile, a combination that Georgiana thought promising. But in six months she knew that no matter how apt the scholars, a prevailing lack of ambition overcast all serious attempts at educational advancement.

When her contract was up for renewal, Georgiana declined, packed up her boxes, and returned to Alton and the home of Moses Atwood.

She thought that if she had a job in a free state, it would be possible to teach pupils that included the Negro race. With this goal in mind, Georgiana placed an advertisement in the *Anti-Slavery Standard* and was promptly offered a position in Columbus, Ohio. Fortified with letters from Eliza Farnham and George Ripley, the teacher prepared to journey once again.

Columbus was due to become another disappointment. Funding for public school education in Ohio was appropriated only for those children at least three-fifths white. If she took the job, Georgiana would be expected to judge the skin color of her pupils by making comparisons with tinted cards. "No exposition of the good I might do to mezzo tints or quadroons could reconcile me to the half-way right," she said.[30]

Outraged, she returned to the East a confirmed abolitionist. She attended anti-slavery meetings in Philadelphia and, among other teaching jobs, taught French and German to several mulatto pupils. She heard the lectures of Lucretia Mott in the Quaker meeting houses and found her imagination inspired by the "Underground" through which the Quakers passed fugitive slaves on their way to safer territory.

Georgiana's zeal for abolitionist reform secured her a job as governess to the children of Robert Purvis in Byberry, fifteen miles from Philadelphia. A man of Scottish descent on his father's side, Purvis had inherited Negro blood through his mother, and he embraced strong abolitionist sentiments. In later years, Georgiana counted him among her most loyal friends.

She was happy in Byberry and remained there eighteen

months before moving to New York. Here she received a letter from
Eliza Farnham, who asked her to come to California and live on a
two-hundred-acre farm in the small, isolated community of Santa
Cruz.

In May of 1850—with a loan from Horace Greeley—
Georgiana made up her mind to head West. Observing the
spreading infection of "gold fever," she later described the
westward preoccupation as a "harmless epidemic, which induced
men of all classes to believe that with a pick and shovel they
could, in a short time, secure a fortune for themselves, or for those
they loved."[31]

"Everywhere that men congregated there would be more or
less sickness," Georgiana concluded. "I had a natural gift for
nursing, why should I not make it avail me, so that I might become
a sharer in the general prosperity?"[32]

Georgiana and Eliza were kindred souls with similar
talents and an equal enthusiasm for reform. Now Mrs. Farnham
promised her younger friend a taste of the wealth she had found in
California; it was a rich opportunity to test new skills and achieve
great changes within the society of the western frontier. Both
women were drawn to the prospects of winning acclaim for
accomplishing goals aimed at the good of society. California was
irresistible.

II. *The* People of the Place, 1850–1864

Georgiana Bruce and Eliza Farnham had worked together for one year at Sing Sing, parting only a short time before Eliza lost her position as the prison matron. Although the theories Eliza introduced helped to improve conditions for the inmates, they were unfavorably received by some of the prison staff, particularly the chaplain. Finally, there was an election of a new board of inspectors in 1848, and the prison matron was forced to resign. During the next two years, while Georgiana had struggled with personal challenges as a teacher, Eliza had been drawn into a whirlpool of national excitement. The gold rush was on and thousands migrated West, to the one place where the roles of womanhood were as yet undefined, where women could stake a claim to equality.

Mrs. Farnham had moved from the prison environment at Sing Sing to the quieter atmosphere of Boston, where she worked with Samuel Gridley Howe at the Perkins Institution and assisted with the education of the famous blind deaf-mute Laura Bridgman.[1]

In these days there was little contact between Eliza and her wandering husband Thomas Farnham. Their relationship had soured, and he had once again gone West, this time to settle permanently in California. She was now a thirty-four-year-old mother with two young sons and a full career. Although she believed women were obligated to improve society through their duties as wives and mothers, Eliza was clearly captivated by her own dreams as an adventuress and by the vision of western independence.

It was also in the summer of 1848 that, coincidentally, the first women's rights convention was held at Seneca Falls, New York. The aims of that convention, the appeal of the frontier, and her own beliefs on the powers of women all served to inspire Mrs. Farnham.[2]

She had already tasted the more unrestrained lifestyles of the Midwest and had warm recollections of her years in Illinois, where she witnessed the developing customs and institutions of western democracy. She was now ready to try California. All she needed was the opportunity, and it came quite suddenly with the news that her husband had died in San Francisco. He had succumbed to fever that September and left Eliza with a law firm and freighting business to dispose of in the city, plus several parcels of land near the state capital at San Jose. In addition, there was a small ranch of some two-hundred acres near the ruins of the Mission Santa Cruz on Monterey Bay.[3]

Eliza had a plan—to civilize the western territory with the superior influence of women and to achieve "some greater good" through her own travels. Within six months of Thomas's death, Eliza issued a printed circular in New York, announcing her intended departure for California and the formation of the "California Association of American Women."[4]

She knew of the conflict in California between the land-wealthy Californios and the overwhelmingly male, gold-hungry, Yankee population. She knew that life in the mines was crude and that men outnumbered women fifty-to-one. At some point, the dust would settle and new communities would appear. Anglo women of all descriptions were greatly desired. What a difference it would make, she reasoned, if the first to arrive were scholarly, chaste, and honorable.

The reformist was convinced that such women would be "one of the surest checks upon the many evils" in mining country. The emigration plan called for more than one hundred "intelligent, virtuous and efficient" women over twenty-five years to accompany Eliza westward on the vessel *Angelique*. She intended to begin the 13,000-mile voyage around Cape Horn in mid-April, 1849.

Each prospective passenger was asked to provide evidence of her background, education, and character. The fare was $250, enough to cover the price of the trip plus the cost of initial accommodations in San Francisco, the point where the ladies would leave Eliza's charge.

A circular was distributed with endorsements from such prominent New Englanders as Horace Greeley, Henry Ward Beecher, William Cullen Bryant, Caroline Kirkland, and writer Catharine M. Sedgwick, who said in her admiration of Eliza, "She has nerves to explore alone the seven circles of Dante's Hell."[5]

Word of the brideship plan blazed across the continent and set aflame the desire of miners who longed for women of a marriageable kind.   They wholeheartedly embraced Eliza's scheme, although most were barely aware of her intent to bring stability and decorum to their rough settlements.   They only rejoiced that she was to bring Yankee women within their grasp; they cared not at all what kind.

She seemed assured of success. The applicants numbered more than two hundred in a short time. But the staid society of New England also misinterpreted Eliza's noble intentions, even though it did clearly perceive the miners' eagerness and outright lust. The proper Easterners called Eliza's brainstorm an immoral ploy and hinted that it was perhaps only a cover for prostitution. Mrs. Farnham, verbally stoned with jeers and gossip, was taken aback by the insinuations and insensitivity. She knew her scruples to be of the purest standard and saw the attack on her character as a humiliating insult.

For several months Eliza ignored the scandalous talk as best she could as she furthered her preparations to sail. Greeley and other friends continued to boost the enterprise, calling the scheme "an errand of mercy to the golden land." In the *Tribune* Greeley described the quest as one evincing moral courage and deserving of the blessings of her countrymen. The supporters of Eliza's plan realized that much of the reaction came because it was a woman, a headstrong advocate of women's rights, who intended to lead it. The proposition itself was out of the normal bounds of female thinking.

Westerners remained enthusiastic, however. On June 7, 1849, the *Alta California* of San Francisco ran a letter from Boston that seemed to illustrate a general zest for the whole idea. "It would not surprise me if Mrs. Farnham obtained as many women in

Lowell to go round the Horn with her as would fill a ship of eight hundred tons," the writer said.[6]

Three days later, a miner noted in his diary that he had attended church three times in one day with the hope of meeting a single woman. "A few ladies present. Does my eye good to see a woman once more," he said. "Hope Mrs. Farnham will bring 10,000."[7]

But the months of sarcasm eventually wore Eliza down. An illness gave her the chance to escape the ridicule and the terms of her obligation. She departed on the *Angelique* accompanied only by her two children, a companion named Miss Sampson, a nursemaid, and two young ladies (who did well for themselves in California, but still decided to go home after only a short stay).

On the trip around Cape Horn, Eliza was soon in conflict with the ship's captain. He retaliated against her stubborn demands with an underhanded trick that left her stranded ashore without baggage or money in a small port on the coast of Chile. Everything precious to Eliza sailed on to San Francisco aboard the *Angelique* . It took the shocked and angry Mrs. Farnham more than a month to catch up on another boat. During this time, her sons Charles and Edward occupied all her thoughts.

Meanwhile, the *Angelique* anchored in San Francisco to the attentions of expectant bachelors who lined the docks to cheer Mrs. Farnham. There were near riots when the promised cargo of eligible ladies failed to appear. When the other passengers disembarked, Miss Sampson and the boys remained aboard and waited. They were finally rescued from the ship after an extended stay of forty-seven days. Enraged, Eliza sought vengeance against the *Angelique's* captain, but a lawsuit was totally unsuccessful. By the time she settled her husband's debts and took care of all business in San Francisco, Eliza was more than ready to depart the city. She shuddered at the fate of so many of the women who lived the fast life in a boom town. She wrote:

> At that period in the history of San Francisco, it was so rare to see a female, that those whose misfortune it was to be obliged to be abroad felt themselves uncomfortably stared at. Doorways filled instantly, and little islands in the streets were thronged with men who seemed to gather

in a moment, and who remained immovable till the spectacle passed from their incredulous gaze. Bold-faced unfortunates, whose presence added infinitely to the discomfort one felt in those dreadful times, were occasionally to be seen in bar-rooms, or, perhaps, hatless and habitless on horseback in the streets, or the great gaming-houses that never were emptied of their throngs.[8]

Eliza further confided that now that she had "experienced the moral and social poverty of the country," she was indeed grateful after all that her brideship plan had failed. "It would be a painful responsibility, which I could never throw off, if I had to reflect that there were persons here through my instrumentality who were less happy or good than they might have been remaining at home," she said.[9]

It was Eliza's first goal in California to become a farmer. She had accurately predicted the fertility of California soil from the moment she set foot on the beach in Santa Cruz. The county was brand new when she landed in February 1850, herself and all her belongings dumped into surf boats, doused with saltwater, and spewed ashore. The name of the place was then "Branciforte County," a title shed within a matter of months and which Eliza herself never used.

"We had come down from San Francisco by sea," she wrote, "been landed like bales of goods through the surf, partly in boats and partly in the arms of the seamen...."[10]

She had to pay $25 for each ship-to-shore delivery of her belongings, plus $8 for every wagonload driven to her ranch. She herself walked the two miles with her children and took her first look at the slopes behind the old mission potrero and the land that was now her home.

Eliza and the community she arrived in greeted one another with more-or-less equal expressions of shock. Santa Cruz was then one of the most isolated, hard-to-reach regions of the entire state. There were no wharves for disembarking passengers, no bridges to link the generally poor roads, and as yet no clear path over the mountains (a situation to be remedied in part by Eliza herself when she became one of the first Yankees to cross the summit to the Santa Clara Valley on a mule trail. For more than a century "Farnham

Road" was named for her.).

Most able-bodied men of the town had gone to the mines at the start of the gold rush. The remaining English-speaking population was tiny and uncultured, particularly to the tastes and customs of one of New England's intellectual elite. The Santa Cruz population, on the other hand, had known of Eliza and was acquainted with Thomas Farnham and his role in retrieving Isaac Graham from Mexico in 1841.[11] The citizenry was little prepared, however, for the sassy, high-bred widow who announced her intentions of becoming a farmer. Nor could they relate to her as a writer, phrenologist, abolitionist, and women's rights advocate— particularly as one with such outspoken opinions.

Eliza was excited about the surroundings of her new community until the moment she saw the Rancho Tres Ojos de Agua and the homesite of "El Rancho La Libertad." It bore little resemblance to her mental pictures.

> See us, after a walk of two miles, on the 22nd of February, through clover and grass four inches [feet?] high, borne down by the heavy dews that had fallen on the previous night, enter the casa of El Rancho La Libertad. There have been two men occupying it before our arrival, who are to remove in the afternoon or the next day. Their household goods consist of a table—the roughest of its species—two or three old benches, three or four bowls, as many plates, and one or two articles of hollow-ware. The casa is not a cheerful specimen even of California habitations—being made of slabs, which were originally placed upright, but which have departed sadly from the perpendicular in every direction. There is not a foot of floor, nor a pane of glass, nor a brick, nor anything in the shape of a stove. The fire is made upon the ground, and the smoke departs by any avenue that seemeth to itself good, or lingers in the airy space between our heads and the roof, which is beautifully done in bas relief of webs, dressed in pyroligneous acid.[12]

Eliza's writings detail her many frustrations as she directed reconstruction of the "casa," while at the same time she attempted to plant virgin ground without harness or plow. The first fragile buds were attacked by grasshoppers and trampled by cattle. Her earliest shipment of trees arrived dead, and another cargo of vitally needed supplies simply disappeared into the surf. Fortified with scanty materials, little knowledge, and even less money, she approached the local work force to hire laborers. Eliza was chagrined at the small pool of workers and the prices they demanded. All the best had gone to the mines, and it was the curse of the farmer, she said, that labor was so hard to find. Those of skill who did remain in town were unaffordable, and all acted as if even the slightest chore was performed as a great favor.

> In California, the relation that elsewhere exists between employer and employed is reversed. The man who does not know but he might make a hundred dollars per day at the mines is not likely to engage with you at two or three dollars, without causing you to feel, from time to time, the favor he confers by staying. Most of the floating laborers to be picked up at this time, were either too infirm in health to be able to go to the mines, or too intemperate to trust themselves there. Invalids, or drunken sailors, were the staple of the laboring community.[13]

There were no illustrated instructional booklets to guide her in the successful techniques of western farming, no seasoned hands to steer her in those early fruitless attempts. During those first months, she was to be "harder at work...than any Southern slave—books, pen, thinking, talking—all as utterly given up as if I were an Esquimaux woman in her ice hut."[14]

Once Eliza scavenged the needed equipment for farming, she slowly rebuilt the casa, settled her family, and then made ambitious plans to construct new and more spacious quarters. She was lent "a splendid saddle horse" with the fitting name of "Sheik" and in stolen moments began to pace the countryside—observing, analyzing, and writing. Eventually she roamed far enough north to see and describe the mining country, although her best assessments of California life were those made closest to home.

Since she was, herself, "of the late emigration," Mrs. Farnham was always the least charitable with other Yankees. None escaped the scrutiny of her notebook and pen. She was the most critical of those who came before the gold rush—the Anglos who took up the native Californio's way of life. These men had often married into ranchero families in order to gain title to the Mexican land grants, vast sections that extended to thousands of acres. She blamed them for "seeking nothing superior to the old rancho style—a dark, dirty, adobe house, windowless, swarming with fleas, the ground in all directions strewn with bullocks' heads, horns, and hides...."[15]

The more recent settlers, however, were judged to be generally illiterate, wholly lacking cultural refinements, and totally obsessed with the pursuit of wealth. Once during a Methodist Church meeting Eliza took stock of the young girls of Santa Cruz. "Nearly all were characterized," she noted, "by that freedom, strength, and self-reliance that belong only to the children of the Western States, and to the ruder conditions of society in which they are born and reared. Their styles of dress were as various as their persons, agreeing in only one feature, that of skirts falling to the feet," she added. "Hideous bonnets, of all fashions, which their grandmothers might have worn, deformed their heads and concealed their fine faces; gowns pinned at the waist in front; monstrous shoes, or may be none at all, showed the want of supplies in the country, if it also argued some lack of taste in its inhabitants."[16]

The price Eliza paid for such caustic remarks was exclusion and rejection. Her attitude was superior, morally righteous, and totally tiresome to the community around her. She soon had to admit that she'd become her own captive. People left her alone.

> The isolation of this period was its most disheartening feature. Shut up in my narrow house, with the interest and sympathies which had been wont to embrace classes, communities, humanity, chilled and driven back upon myself; unable to approach the social life about me in the way of co-operation or enjoyment, or individuals in the relation of serving or aiding, because their wants were not those to which I could minister, I was, most of all, unhappy in finding myself circumscribed in all action to my small family circle and my private interests. The least endowed and cultivated woman in the community was more valuable to it, if she had health and industry, than I had power to be. Her fitness to serve society in its

> primitive conditions, to supply its first wants, made her
> superior in the things wherein excellence can be
> practically tested, and gave her sources of happiness,
> which, surrounded as I was, I could not command.[17]

Eliza conceded in the end of that first year that her
superlative philosophical insights, so admired in New England,
were worthless when applied to the practical and physical
demands of western living. She thought women on this coast were
to be freer and of a purer intellect than men; she found these
attributes neither desired nor appreciated.

"There is little in the condition of California society, up to
this date, to engage the higher orders of female intelligence, and,
among all earnest women of this class whom I have met, there is a
universal feeling of being sadly out of place," she added.[18]

Eliza then gave a strong piece of advice to other New
Englanders who might contemplate a western adventure:

> The necessities to be served here are physical; washing
> linen, cleansing houses, cooking, nursing, etc., and I would
> advise no woman to come alone to the country who has not
> strength, willingness, and skill for one or other of these
> occupations; who has not, also, fortitude, indomitable
> resolution, dauntless courage, and a clear self-respect
> which will alike forbid her doing anything unworthy
> herself, or esteeming anything to be so, which her
> judgment and conscience approve.... She will feel herself
> in an enemy's country, where she is to watch and ward
> with tireless vigilance, and live, unless she be very
> happily circumstanced, alone, entirely alone, and bear
> her trials in silence. None but the pure and strong-hearted
> of my sex should come alone to this land.[19]

Mrs. Farnham's desperation and loneliness could only be
ended by an ally—someone as keenly tuned as she to the
refinements of the reformist elite, yet more a diplomat, too,
capable of tact and restraint of tongue. That friend was Georgiana
Bruce, who sent a note from San Francisco and arrived at just the
right moment to assuage Eliza's pride and redeem her spirit of
excitement.

Attracted by promises of financial security as a teacher and farmer, Georgiana rode horseback from San Francisco on a journey no less harrowing than Eliza's own landing in Santa Cruz. "Geordie" (a name for Georgiana coined by Eliza's son, Eddie) arrived wet, chilled, and starved after a night stranded in the mountains without food or shelter. Eliza hardly allowed her time for recovery before pressing for news of happenings in the East:

> There were endless tidings to be heard—as Geordie had left home a year after my departure—of coteries; of societies; of individuals; of late books; of reform movements; of successes and failures; of marriages, births, deaths; of Eastern friends, and the Western set—in short, of the thousand persons, events, and subjects in whom and which my interest was almost painfully revived by the presence of one fresh from among them.[20]

In her isolation, Eliza ached for details of the anti-slavery movement, prison reformers, phrenological techniques, and spiritualism; of new authors, editors, developments in women's education. She quizzed Georgiana till they were both exhausted. "I was no more alone now, nor lonely; for, what with personal reminiscences, discussions of social, religious, and moral questions, and analyses of character, we had few dull or silent hours."[21]

Georgiana and Eliza delighted in one another's company, rediscovering their similarities and relishing the solidarity of their reformist philosophies. Georgiana's arrival that summer of 1850 was to redirect their lives and, ultimately, their relationship to each other. Because Georgiana had a slightly less rigid and more gentle demeanor and a better sense of discretion, she was able to do what Eliza had been powerless to achieve—slowly, the two connected with Santa Cruz social and religious circles. They entered the routines of community life, although both were still considered eccentrics with odd behavior and radical, perhaps, even dangerous, ideas.

Shedding petticoats for Turkish pants, they took hammer and nails in hand as the carpenters of Eliza's new home. When she began construction, Eliza succeeded so well that she "laughed, whenever I paused for a few moments to rest, at the idea of promising to pay a man $14 or $16 per day for doing what I found my own hands so dexterous in."[22]

Bursting with confidence and bravado, the women addressed letters to mutual friends in New England, the phrenologist-publishers, Fowler and Wells. Addressing her letter to Mrs. Wells, Georgiana spoke of the perverted influences in the West, but at the same time she flaunted the freedoms of her more adventuresome lifestyle.

> Now here we are—that is Mrs. Farnham & myself—in the midst of most beautiful nature but entirely cut off from the aid to progress wh[ic]h is afforded by the society of ones *equals* even.[23]

Eliza asked for books on a number of topics, but was particularly interested in the subject of spiritualism and the messages of the séance. (She was perhaps hopeful that visitations by departed intellectuals could help fill the cultural void in Santa Cruz.) In her letter, Georgiana made mention of Eliza's special zeal for this new passion. Perhaps she was aware, even then, that spiritualism was to be the one sin the local population would persecute with mockery and ostracism. Georgiana continues:

> As for me *I* am in excellent health & spirits &, notwithstanding that I do not think transplanting onions to be fancy work I intend to brave it out & shall remain in Santa Cruz for some years certainly. I have never regretted coming—not even when I was living on short meals with a long grace at the deplorable washing establishment where I ironed shirts, cooked & slept on the kitchen floor for $75 per month & now that I luxuriate in the unparalled [sic] freedom of turkish pants & tunic with frequent rides on horseback—not forgetting the onions, regret would be equivalent to apostacy. By the way it is my belief that this modification of the Turkish & Albanian dress which Mrs F & I find so convenient will eventually become the fashion here for you see we are amenable to no vulgar public opinion &—I say it with all due modesty—we are *the* people of the place—live more like civilised beings than anyone else & if anything

worthy *does* come to S. C. it comes to our house. There is
one other woman & only one who is not a wooden spoon
(bass wood at that) & she has engaged me to fix her some
dresses & her husband has always wished her to dress so.
After six months freedom from petticoats you will permit
me to say that you don't know what you suffer.[24]

Eliza's letter to Fowler and Wells was dated November 15,
1850. Her tone was less complacent, and her comments were blended
with an appreciative narrative of her surroundings. Her writing is
optimistic, still bold, and yet, almost fragile:

My farm is a mile and a half from the Beach on which
the sounding surf breaks, making glorious music day &
night. The neighborhood is settling rapidly with a good
class of Western people chiefly Methodists.   Their
Minister is a self-educated and tolerably intelligent man
who studied Phrenology & taught it before he went to
College to prepare for the ministry. His early studies
have somewhat counteracted the virulence of theology
but he rants occasionally of fire and brimstone. There is a
charming community of young girls here 40 in number and
Miss Bruce is to open a girls school with us next week. She
fills up a great place in my dark world and comes to me
like a pleasant breeze or a bright sun after one of our long
rains. We are going to be very independent and free here
wearing the Albanian Costume and dashing about at our
discretion. I have been building a house literally with
my own hands this summer—a pretty cottage with little
spires and gables over the windows. It is not done yet but I
hope to have it finished in Eastern style in the course of
the next six mo.[25]

Eliza made one comment to Fowler and Wells that was
prophetic of her later hardships. It was as if she knew, even
unconsciously, that land ownership was her Achilles' heel—a
privilege allowed western women although not yet defended under
law. Still, this was a more advanced foothold than on the East
Coast, where laws generally forbade females the right to property
title. In her letter, Mrs. Farnham listed two-hundred acres that
she owned in Santa Cruz, plus two-hundred at Mission St. Joseph's,

and three-hundred to five-hundred more near the State Capital at San Jose. It was her wish that profits from these lands would allow a steady income for herself and her sons.

"It is no easy thing for a woman to defend property here," she added. "She may get it more easily than any where else in Christendom but all things are so unsettled and baseless that when one has property one must be ever on the alert to see that it is not taken from them, a watch that is not easy for a woman to keep up."[26]

It was important then for both Eliza and Georgiana to give their friends the impression that life was a *savoir faire* adventure. In truth, Eliza's troubles in the community grew increasingly worse. She had already been talked out of the bulk of her money by one male "friend," and now she had invited one of the hired hands, an Irishman named Thomas Russell, to take over management of the farm.

Russell had a brother who ran the file factory at Sing Sing Prison. It was through this connection, perhaps, that he sought out Eliza for a job soon after his arrival in San Francisco from the mines. Russell also helped entice Georgiana to Santa Cruz with exaggerated accounts of Eliza's wealth and the existing opportunities for success in farming.[27]

It has remained unclear precisely how Russell engineered his claim on Eliza's lands. Neither are there any exact details about Georgiana's involvement; but whatever happened, it destroyed the intimacy the two women had enjoyed that first year. The bitterness is plainly expressed in part of Georgiana's initial journal entry, dated December 14, 1852:

> I had grown old in fretting about Mrs. Farnham's troubles and perplexities. She was so ignorant of business, so careless, so easily imposed on, and at the same time so determined to get so much under weigh at once that she was constantly in debt or in hot water somehow. She let Buckle, who had $7000 of her husband's money, persuade her to set up farming without any title. He presently failed—she took Russell, an Irishman, without self-respect, without system, without knowledge of how to treat or deal with men and with no idea of straight-

forwardness, of speaking the truth—simply a skillful and
industrious worker, and trusted to him management of her
farm in Santa Cruz. After that she took a half-fool, half-
knave (Pelton) who did no better. Then she married the
greatest blackguard in the country who strikes and
otherwise ill treats her. At the time I write she has
returned to him for the second time. Her children are
tossed about here and there and her property wholly
unattended to and unproductive.[28]

The trouble may have started the previous spring. Santa
Cruz County records show that Eliza and Georgiana were both
married to local settlers on March 23, 1852. Eliza became the bride
of the Irish immigrant, William Alexander Fitzpatrick, a man
known for his violent temper. Georgiana exchanged vows with
another native of England, Richard C. Kirby. He had jumped a
whaling ship off Puget Sound in 1845, and was now owner of a
prospering tannery in Santa Cruz. (See Journal, note 2.)

Eliza's ceremony was formally witnessed by Russell. On
that day, she also deeded over to him portions of the farm at a
price of $7,000. The Kirbys were involved, too, since their names
were recorded on contracts of the same date. Years later, Richard
acted as attorney for both himself and Eliza in court battles over
Eliza's claim to Rancho Tres Ojos de Agua. They lost to Russell's
heirs.[29]

It may have been at this time that the lives of these
friends took irreversible shifts. Georgiana became more secure,
while Eliza suffered a series of tragic blows. The discord between
them is traceable only to Eliza's mismanagement of money and her
choice of a mate, although part of Georgiana's anger may have
come from her awareness that they no longer shared a common
destiny.

The alienation lasted more than a year, before loneliness
and the births of two baby girls brought them back together. On
June 29, 1853, Georgiana noted in her journal that she and Eliza had
given birth within four days of one another. Their first visit
afterwards had included the application of phrenological
measurements to each child, and that intellectual exchange alone
was enough to mend the relationship.

"I love Mrs. F. in spite of the anxiety and trouble she has caused us and may yet, by her past culpable action," admitted Georgiana. "How I long for a more intellectual life."[30]

In Santa Cruz, no positive words (save those of Georgiana) were ever given to Mrs. Farnham. She earned no testimonial in the early biographical sketches devoted to venerated pioneers. Most of the comments she received were caustic (one critic branded her a "She Devil"). By 1855, she could no longer endure the mockery. Her youngest son, Edward, had succumbed to a long illness, and this tragedy was soon followed by the death of her infant daughter. Eliza's attempts to teach and lecture in the local community were continually opposed by church and social leaders. And all this happened while she tolerated the abuses of her husband. It was time to leave.

On July 5, 1856, the *Sentinel* recorded the divorce proceedings of "Farnham versus Fitzpatrick." Her charges of extreme cruelty were found "sufficient and legal cause to obtain a decree of divorce." It was one of the first in the county. On this one occasion the local paper noted that Eliza was "distinguished as a lecturer and well-known in every part of the nation."[31]

The reformist toured the state once again before returning to New York City to publish the book about her California experiences. Once again in the company of friends in an intellectual community, her energy and interest in the women's rights movement were ignited. She drew upon the subjects of art, history, religion, philosophy, and biology to substantiate her views in a book she titled *Woman and Her Era*, a work dedicated to Georgiana Kirby. It was this treatise that firmly asserted Eliza's belief in the superiority of the female sex.[32]

It was Eliza's theory that the oppression of women stemmed from men's subconscious realization that the female sex was created for a higher and more refined purpose than the male. Eliza cited the reproductive role of women as evidence and argued that it was a creative power second only to that of God. It was man's duty, therefore, to provide the physical environment to support women's status as the superior being.

On May 13, 1858, Eliza carried her ideas to the platform of the National Women's Rights Convention in New York City. She spoke alongside the movement's leaders, calling for the dawn of a "higher era" to place women in their true positions as the holders of nobler virtues. It was beneath women, she implied, to strive for equality with an inferior sex.[33]

Mrs. Farnham made one last visit to Santa Cruz in 1859 and then took a job briefly, from 1861 to 1862, as the matron of the female department of the Insane Asylum at Stockton, California. When she returned to New York in 1862, she joined the Women's Loyal National League and was among the abolitionists who petitioned Congress to end slavery through Constitutional amendment.[34]

As she neared her 44th birthday, Eliza was finally more at peace with herself. Georgiana commented in her journal how much the activist's features had softened, giving her a more attractive and less harsh appearance. Now that her one surviving son, Charles, had reached manhood, the women's rights advocate was more in harmony with her own opinions. There was less need to prove her own worth in motherhood. During this time, Eliza completed two more books: *Eliza Woodson,* a fictional work about her own painful childhood (originally published in 1859 as *My Early Days*), and *The Ideal Attained*, a fictional explanation of her ideas on manhood and womanhood. She had taken up studies of medicine at the start of the Civil War and then in the winter of 1863, she answered the call for volunteer nurses to serve on the battlefields.

Eliza worked with the wounded at Gettysburg, serving until she herself became ill. She contracted tuberculosis and died in New York City on December 15, 1864, at the age of forty-nine.

An article in the *Sentinel* recorded her death in New York, but there was no eulogy. Instead, the paper couldn't resist one last sarcastic jab. The story recalled her spiritualist interests as well as her short employment at the insane asylum. Her death would allow her to converse at length with her spiritualist followers here, the writer joked, and such ethereal talks would no doubt provide additional inmates within the asylum walls.[35]

However, national women's rights leaders later remembered Eliza with a more gentle, reverent view:

> The advocacy of women's rights began in Santa Cruz
> County with the advent of that grand champion of her

sex, the immortal Eliza Farnham, who braved public scorn because of her advanced views for so many years before the suffrage movement assumed an organized form. Mrs. Farnham's work rendered it possible for those advocating women suffrage years later to do so with comparative immunity from public ridicule.

This was the tribute given Eliza in the *History of Woman Suffrage,* edited by Susan B. Anthony, Elizabeth Cady Stanton, and Matilda Joslyn Gage.[36]

More praise was given about the same time by novelist Helen Hunt Jackson. In her book *Bits of Travel at Home* (1878), the author devoted several pages to the place she called "Holy Cross Village." However, what begins as a description of the town quickly becomes a testimonial to Eliza and Georgiana and the courageous lives they lived together in Santa Cruz. Writing of Eliza, she said:

> The farm on which she and her beloved friend, Georgia [sic] Bruce, toiled like men, and sowed and reaped and builded with their own hands, lies little more than a mile away from the town. Mrs. Farnham's house was burnt down, a short time ago; but another has been built on the same spot.... When that adventurous woman broke ground for her house, no other house was in sight, except the Mission Building, and the little shanty in which she lived while her own house was going up.... On the day that we were there, men were tossing hay in the beautiful, curving meadow hollows just before the house,—the same meadow where Mrs. Farnham sowed the first wheat which was sowed in Santa Cruz, and where Georgia[sic] Bruce spent whole days in planting potatoes. The air was almost heavy with the fragrance from the fresh hay.... Hardship and struggle seem monstrous in such an atmosphere. There must have been an air of mockery to those toiling pioneers in the very smile of this transcendently lovely Nature. To want bread, to need shelter in such realms of luxuriance and warmth; to suffer, to die under such skies,—the heart resents and rejects the very thought with passionate disbelief. But such thoughts, such recollections, such

struggle, are, after all, the needed shadow to a too vivid sun. Holy Cross Village is blessed of both,—blessed in its sparkling sea, its rainless sky, its limitless blossom; blessed also in the memory of Eliza Farnham, and the presence to-day of Georgia[sic] Bruce Kirby.[37]

III. The Muse of Santa Cruz, 1865–1887

Georgiana's friendship with Eliza cast the role she was to assume in Santa Cruz. Georgiana was always to be a respected and yet conspicuously different member of cultured society. Her community stature was influential and made secure by both her successful marriage to tannery owner Richard Kirby and her own developing role as the mother of five children.

It was her intellectual prowess that kept her somewhat apart in certain circles and gave her an even more weighty command in others. People feared Georgiana. She was stubborn, opinionated, and determined about specific issues. In particular, she looked down on those who were intolerant. She never found it necessary or even desirable to be condescending or contrite to please her neighbors. Even the most upstanding pioneer fathers, the financial, political, and social leaders of Santa Cruz, knew better most of the time than to enter verbal or literary arenas with Georgiana.

Her unique position made her a natural spearhead in many causes. In some ways, she took privileges not typically afforded to women. It was an attitude nutured during her first days with Eliza, and one she never gave up. Time after time, Georgiana wrote and spoke about the issues she thought important. And when she offered her view, it was seldom overlooked or discounted. Her statements regarding the subjects of education, temperance, and women's rights appeared in local papers with such regularity that Georgiana was at times a staff writer on these topics.

When Eliza left Santa Cruz, Georgiana inherited a legacy

to watch after the developing roles for women. She remained faithful to this responsibility and shared her interpretations with a widespread audience through the press. By doing so, Georgiana herself narrates much of the last chapter of feminist activism in nineteenth-century Santa Cruz County.

It might have been simpler to concentrate on family life and to suppress her passion for human rights in the decade of the 1860's. But the Civil War and her anti-slavery stand, along with memories of teaching in the Southern border states of Missouri and Illinois, combined to keep her interest alive and caused her to write a letter to the *Anti-Slavery Standard,* published on November 30, 1869, in which she said:

> Inspite of our much vaunted climate, the wheat crops, and even the *Overland Monthly* it takes a long time for an adopted Californian to become acclimated. We suffer, not like the Englishman in New York, from "same sickness" produced by the monotony of the always repeated blocks of houses, but from what may be called "non-cohesion." We have torn up the roots that fastened us to our old homes, old associates, and cautiously put down slender fibres into the new soil. Hence in full possession of wheat, grapes, and the *Overland,* we are conscious of faintness, starvation, at times. Only the children are healthy and happy...Cliques are numerous, and friendships few. I read the beloved *Standard,* a companion of twenty-five years; read therein accounts of radical clubs in Boston, of social science conventions, and Freedom's schools. I sigh to think that our isolated position and our unassimilated population forbid our participation in similar activities.

Although still removed from the cause-oriented stimulation of the East Coast, Georgiana nonetheless took full advantage of the enlightened few she found in Santa Cruz. And where an open-minded attitude toward human rights existed, Georgiana coaxed it toward a greater acceptance of women's rights as well.

Georgiana was a tactician and lobbyist. Always linked to the women's rights movement in the East, she took it upon herself to encourage the ranks in the West. She was the founder, in 1869, of the first local society of suffragists. Within a year, this group convinced an impressive list of local residents to sign a statewide petition to the California legislature. Some of the county's most honored citizens were among more than two hundred who signed, and no doubt many did so under Georgiana's influence. Included on the list were such well-known names as Majors, Hecox, Case, Blackburn, and a score of other early pioneering families, all asking the legislature for an amendment "to secure to the women of this commonwealth the right of suffrage."

There were two names on the petition worthy of particular note—Captain Albert Brown, the Santa Cruz County Clerk, and Mrs. Ellen Van Valkenburg, widow of San Lorenzo Paper Mill founder Henry Van Valkenburg. These two Santa Cruz citizens were soon to take primary roles in a well-planned citizen action carefully coordinated with the arrival in Santa Cruz of national suffragist leaders. It was an event thoroughly masterminded and reported by Georgiana.

Inspired by the victory of the 1869 territorial suffrage bill in Wyoming that allowed women for the first time the right to vote, the local society of women's rights advocates decided that year to stage a challenge of California voting laws. The argument was based upon the Fourteenth and Fifteenth Amendments to the Constitution.

The action began when Mrs. Van Valkenburg went to County Clerk Brown, an accomplice in the scheme, and demanded to sign the voting register. She claimed this right on grounds that she had been a county taxpayer and the sole support of her children since her husband died nearly a decade before. Captain Brown formally refused and then initiated proceedings for the test case of *Van Valkenburg versus Brown*.[1]

The appeal reached the courts at the very moment national suffragists Susan B. Anthony and Elizabeth Cady Stanton arrived in town on a statewide tour. They came at Georgiana's request.

Stanton and Anthony spoke in major cities across the nation. They arrived in San Francisco in mid-summer and stayed at the Grand Hotel, lecturing nightly. California was on the eve of an election, and the activists frequently found themselves sharing the same platforms as the touring politicians John A. Bingham of Ohio and Senator Cornelius Cole of California. Just as often, the issues of discussion were also the same—the Thirteenth, Fourteenth, and Fifteenth Amendments.

The two suffragists were joined in San Francisco by a third, Emily Pitt Stevens, editor of *The Pioneer*, who also applied to register for the vote with the county clerk of San Francisco. When she was refused, she announced her intention to file suit. The action again indicated the close coordination between the national movement and the smaller organizations in the West.

An announcement appeared in the *Santa Cruz Sentinel* in early August, 1871, noting the scheduled lecture of Mrs. Anthony to be held at the Santa Cruz Unity Church.

"At this time when the question 'shall women possess the right to vote in common with the negro' is so widely agitated, it would be well to hear the subject ably discussed by one who represents a large majority of her sex who have no male relatives to represent their views on political matters," the article stated. [2]

Following the suffragist's talk on the "The Power of the Ballot" (a lecture given in both Santa Cruz and Watsonville), the *Santa Cruz Sentinel* reported that "Miss Anthony is a pleasant speaker and said a great many good things, but whether she convinced the audience that the many wrongs which women suffer from the bonds of the tyrant man will be remedied by giving them the ballot, is a question."[3]

The same issue of this paper, dated August 12, 1871, announced that circulars had been distributed regarding "Mrs. Van Valkenburg's Trial" and the anticipated decision of Judge McKee.

An article in the *Watsonville Pajaronian*, appearing about the same time, also gave some sympathy to the cause:

> Mrs. Ellen A. Van Valkenburg, a taxpayer, an American citizen, an old and respected resident of Santa Cruz, who is the honored head of her family, has lately made application to the proper authorities for registration, so as to become a legal voter, and has been refused on account of sex. The matter has been laid before the Court, and will be prosecuted to success, or to the utmost limits of a well contested struggle for "equal rights." The lady who is a writer of growing fame, has enlisted several of the prominent business men in Santa Cruz in her behalf.[4]

These statements mark the degree to which local suffragists had lobbied and gained support for the women's issues. However, by the time Stanton arrived in town to begin her series of lectures on August 19, the judge's decision against Mrs. Van Valkenburg's application was known. The leader came to talk about suffrage, marriage, divorce, and maternity, but immediately turned her comments toward the local appeal.

Introduced to the audience by Captain Brown, Mrs. Stanton immediately questioned the judgement of Judge McKee in his decision. She said:

> I feel somewhat depressed in appearing before you this evening. One of your judges in his decision this week has denied women the right to vote. He stated that in the eye of the civil law we are persons, but in represntation we are not persons, and women have no political rights which men are bound to respect. The women must now take a New Departure, the same as the Democrats in Ohio. Now, the Fourteenth and Fifteenth Amendments decide the question, as to who are citizens. The Fifteenth Amendment says that any person etc., yet your Judge said that women are not persons, and that he could decide no other way. Does such language show him to be a man of sense? It is debasing in a man of his elevated position to use it....[5]

The actual words of Judge McKee, delivered on August 16, were:

> That under the civil law women had certain rights, and were entitled to and received the protection of the law; but this conferred upon them no political rights. The different States had adopted clauses in their Constitutions stating what class of persons were entitled to political rights. In the State of California the right of suffrage was confined to white male, native born and naturalized citizens, who have reached political age, and those who had obtained their political rights under the treaty of Queretaro. Under the Fourteenth Amendment women had their civil rights guaranteed to them, so had the Indians, and male infants, who had not

reached political age, but it conferred on them no political rights. Physically they are persons, politically they are not. The Fifteenth Amendment was a special act, intended to confer political rights upon male Africans, who had been slaves, and was confined strictly to that class of persons. The word sex is not used in the Fifteenth Amendment, but it is in the Fourteenth Amendment, which prohibits any State from denying political rights to any male inhabitant qualified to exercise such rights. But this did not include women, and she did not come within the meaning and intention of the law. Women have never been permitted to take part in the affairs of the government, and in framing the laws, their case was not probably thought of. It was not considered necessary to do so. The counsel would hardly contend that infants had political rights, yet they are persons, and if by the operation of the word person, females may claim the right of suffrage, why not infants also? In order to confer political rights upon women, special legislation will be necessary, in the same manner as has been done in the case of male Africans. I do not think the Fourteenth and Fifteenth Amendments confer any political rights upon women. I deny the application.[6]

Susan B. Anthony, Elizabeth Cady Stanton, and Emily Pitt Stevens remained in Santa Cruz through August 26, and continued to lecture and offer support to Georgiana and her followers. When she returned East, Mrs. Anthony attempted similar action of her own and was arrested and fined $100 for her illegal vote in the national presidential election.   Years later, when nationwide sympathy was stronger, the famous suffragist met Georgiana's daughter Cornelia while on a visit to Berkeley and told her: "My dear, I visited your mother when they threw rotten eggs at me, now they throw roses."

The August decision of Judge McKee against Mrs. Van Valkenburg's petition was a set-back for the Santa Cruz group, but no reason to give up. The appeal was continued and the case taken to the Supreme Court. It was a difficult move, however, particularly since Mrs. Van Valkenburg herself had left Santa Cruz.

Georgiana's skill as a news writer and the energy and

commitment of local women's rights advocates were best illustrated in a lengthy article that appeared in the *Santa Cruz Sentinel* on September 30, 1871. The article is signed with the initials "G. B. K.," and includes the comments of local suffragists against Judge McKee's decision, as well as an explanation of Ellen Van Valkenburg's departure. The article reads:

> The large attendance at Unity Church on Wednesday evening—the very earnest and dignified character of the addresses made on this occasion, and the respectful attention accorded by the audience to those who advocated woman's equality with man before the law, bore marked evidence in the rapid spread and acceptance of the views set forth.
>
> R. C. Kirby having been voted to the chair—Mrs. Van Valkenburg—whose suit for Registration is carried to the Supreme Court of this State at the approaching term— made a few opening remarks, in explanation of the reasons which had caused her to take the step she had. In 1862, she had become, under the most painful circumstances, a widow—Mr. Van Valkenburg was killed suddenly by the falling of a tree during the great flood of that year—and for ten years she had been obliged to manage her own affairs, pay her own taxes, and struggle along alone to bring up her family. Busy now, in her preparations to leave for the East on the morrow, she had had no time to think of speech-making. She was convinced that what she had done was proper, legitimate, womanly, and she should leave the town where she had suffered and enjoyed so much, in a very hopeful state of mind; believing that the work which was now definitely commenced, would, in a short time, be crowned with success.
>
> Mrs. Larkin, in a calm, deliberate and kindly manner, set before the audience, a picture of how long men had consented to live under the rule of despots, to be governed by kings and emperors with no voice in the laws that govern them. When first the ideas of free-speech, free-thought, liberty and justice began to be agitated among them, only a few of the most daring, ventured to enlist in the cause; only a few realized the degrading effects of

subserviency.

After long centuries of oppression, at last the blood of our forefathers freely poured out in the cause of liberty, secured to them their freedom—the right of self-government. A decade of years has passed, and now, woman sees that she has the same inalienable rights that man has—the right to be represented in the government; to help make the laws that govern her, and as men formerly did, so she has petitioned again and again, the powers that be for her rights; and now we no longer petition—we *demand* them. These rights existed before government; indeed it would seem that efforts of the latter were directed to governing the many for the benefit of the few—to denying rights. Women have depended on *privilege* too long. Casting aside all fears and pretensions in their united womanhood, and in the strength of systematized co-operation, they *demand* a voice in making the laws that they have to obey.

In getting the Franchise, we shall need to devote our thoughts to the great problems on which depend the well-being of society. We can do this easily as we can waste our powers in the adornment of our person. "The average young woman," says Miss Phelps, the author of *Gates Ajar*—expends enough inventive power; enough financial shrewdness; enough close foresight; perturbation of spirit; presence of mind; patience of hope; anguish of regret, upon one season's outfit, to make an excellent bank cashier, or a good graduate of a Theological Seminary. I want women to have the Franchise that they may be more *womanly*, more earnest and thoughtful; that they be no longer satisfied with putting 237 buttons on a dress, not one of which is of any use, or 425 yards of trimmings—as Dr. Lewis says of another, or be willing to ride from Portland to Boston without leaning back lest she should tumble her sash. I want woman to have the Franchise, that the venerable doors of Harvard and Yale, may swing open to them and the learning and libraries benefit them as well as their brothers. When women have the Franchise, Courts of Law will become truely Courts of Justice, and when woman is dragged in as a criminal, she shall find in the clean, carpeted and comfortable jury-box, intelligent, benevolent women faces, as well as those of men. I want no longer to see woman accused by laws she had no voice in making; tried by judges she had no hand in electing; judged and condemned, or acquitted, by a jury not of her peers. Make woman a political force and she can offset Dr. Holland's infamous bill which proposes to make vice respectable, and to enable the sensualist to deceive the Almighty and evade the penalty of his sin, while the poor, helpless victims of man's lust are to be publicly registered and pay a tax to the government—a christian government! for the privilege of being victims. She can offset this bill with another, which shall make each man visiting these hells, to be registered and his personal appearance described in the daily papers, while he shall pay a tax which shall help to support the broken down outcast as she approaches her early grave.

I want the Franchise for woman so that when she makes a coat just as well as a tailor could, she shall be paid the same sum for her work. For when she buys a barrel of flour, or a cord of wood, there is no female price for either of those articles. Also that when women meet at a dinner party together, they may find subject for conversation better than discussing the moral purity of little school girls.

For man's sake too I wish her to have the ballot. I believe every good man has the right to an intelligent, helpful companion in his wife, instead of a painted, insipid, helpless doll, or drudge, with no opinions of her own; a helpless drag on her husband; an abject creature who is obliged, if you ask 25 cents of her for some humanitarian purpose, or $1 for a book to say with downcast eyes, "You will have to wait till *he* comes home. It will be just as *he* says."

The Fourteenth Amendment says "All persons born, or naturalized in the United States and subject to the jurisdiction thereof, are *citizens*," and "citizens," it says, "have the right to vote." Webster's Dictionary defines "person" to be "an individual human being, consisting of soul and body." Now Mrs. Van Valkenburg is a "person." She is a citizen because she was born in the United States and subject to the jurisdiction thereof. She is guilty of no crime, unless it is a crime to be born a woman. When Judge McKee refused her the Franchise, he acted in defiance of

the Constitution of the United States, which overrules all
State laws.

During the trial to which I allude, our very efficient
counsel said in his argument that "It would be just as
sensible to deny a man the right to vote because he wore a
plug hat as to say a 'person,' a 'citizen,' could not vote on
account of sex."

Mrs. Larkin then proceeded to answer the ordinary
objections to giving suffrage to women:

That woman would neglect household matters.

That she would be obliged to leave her infant and go into
the jury-box; that she would be degraded by descending
into the filthy pool of politics; that it will produce
discord in families—because the husband would never
allow his wife to vote any ticket but his own. Having
easily disposed of these fears, she went on to show that
the Suffrage for woman was now a foregone conclusion and
a year would see the matter settled.   Then would
commence a social revolution, for each woman would no
longer waste her time cooking three meals a day for three
or four persons, and washing every week for the same
number without the aid of machinery when by
combination and a proper division of labor, such as men
have long availed themselves of in other departments,
better cooking could be secured at less expense, and more
skillful laundry work could be had for half, or a quarter
the expenditure of means. Women will then entertain
wiser and loftier ambitions, and will have time to
cultivate their minds and discipline their characters for
nobler uses than to cook three meals a day 365 days in the
year; to keep account of the amount of flour in the barrel;
the tea, sugar, soap, starch, butter, to attend to the
baking, washing, dusting, sweeping, starching, ironing,
folding, making and mending of clothes, washing dishes,
preserving, pickling, canning, drying fruit; because all
these now wearing duties will be rendered easy by some
system of cooperation.

Mrs. Field now took the stand and made a short, clear,
logical, refined statement of woman's constitutional right
to the ballot; paying a well deserved compliment to Hon.
Judge Hagan who has so generously given us his time and
legal ability free of charge. We only regret, that owing to

the low tone, so common with untried speakers, so much of her excellent argument was lost by those farthest from the platform.

Mrs. Armstrong next addressed the meeting in a distinct, pleasant voice, but with rather too hurried a delivery. She had no sympathy with the small party of suffragists who sought to destroy the sanctity of marriage. They were but a handful among the large body of workers, and these latter believe in a marriage of one man with one woman. Neither did she feel inclined to inveigh against the tyranny of man. Men found themselves in this social condition and she believed they were now willing to concede, what the ignorant past had denied to woman. We do not intend to drag woman down to the social and political level at which men assure us they exist; but instead, to elevate men, by demanding that they come up to the same standard they raise for woman—to educate boys in the same refinement the same purity of mind and body, that hitherto we have only thought necessary for our girls.

Mr. Albert Brown then addressed the meeting on the legal status of woman—giving many instances of her helplessness before the unjust laws made by those who claim to be her protectors and representatives; but as we hope to see this speech published entire in next week's Sentinel, we forbear to make extracts.

G. B. K.[7]

When the Supreme Court upheld the decision of Judge McKee and denied women the right to vote, the Santa Cruz suffragists followed with yet one more attempt in the early spring of 1872. This time, a single woman named Nellie C. Tator applied to the Santa Cruz Court for admission to the bar. The court referred the case to committee for investigation, "to ascertain whether the laws of the United States permitted ladies to practice law as attorneys," the Sentinel reported on March 30.[8]

"Now as Judge McKee in his decision of the case of Mrs. Van Valkenburg against Albert Brown, which decision has recently been sustained by the Supreme Court of the United States, stated that women were not citizens under the laws of the United States, we do not see how the committee can do otherwise than report against the application," the reporter concluded.[9]

The challenge for enfranchisement and the application for the bar were unsuccessful, yet still bold moves for women to take in a county so small in territory and population as Santa Cruz. Georgiana and her friends did not get the chance to vote within a year—indeed, most never had the opportunity in their lives at all. Suffragists waited nearly another half-century before the ballot was won.

Santa Cruz women's rights advocates kept on fighting, too, and only shifted the emphasis of their actions in the next decade. Georgiana appears as the leader again just two years later at the start of the temperance crusade of 1874.

Early that spring, a charter amendment, proposed to place an additional tax on liquor dealers, had failed for lack of public awareness. The defeat awakened the social wrath of the women's rights activists, and within a week the Santa Cruz Temperance Union was organized with Mrs. Kirby as spokeswoman. She rallied citizens to the issue with the circulation of a petition that strengthened support for the state and national crusade as well as the local effort.

There was no attempt to limit the general consumption of alcoholic beverages. The thrust of the Temperance Union was against the temptation of public drunkenness—the temptation provided by saloons.

Within months, a state Local Option Law was passed to allow citizens of a community to petition for an election against liquor licensing. If such a measure were successful, retailers would still be permitted to sell liquor in quantities greater than five gallons.

In Santa Cruz, heated battles in local newspapers matched the fervor elsewhere in the state. An election under the new law was held in May, and the campaign of the Santa Cruz Temperance Union was victorious by a narrow margin.

However, the effect upon local saloons was nil. Within two months, the State Supreme Court ruled the law unconstitutional on grounds that the Legislature had delegated too much authority to local communities.

For Georgiana and her temperance advocates, victory was victory. They had entered a political fight for a women's rights issue and won. Such action not only proved their commitment, it confirmed their strength for the future. Such dedication was to be the rich inheritance of Santa Cruz County feminists.

One of the most accurate and candid portrayals of Georgiana Bruce Kirby was made of the suffragist as she entered the last decade of her life. Mary Hallock Foote, a talented Victorian novelist and illustrator, was in 1877 a young woman who had just arrived to join her husband, engineer Arthur D. Foote, in the quicksilver mining district of New Almaden, near San Jose. She was, like Georgiana, a cultured woman, comfortable with upper-class social circles, but also an adventurer fascinated with new dimensions of life in the rural West. During the summer of that year, her husband went to search for a new job in San Francisco while Mrs. Foote chose to go with her newborn child to Santa Cruz for health and climate. She had been introduced to Georgiana through her aunt, who had been active in the anti-slavery and suffrage movements. "In Santa Cruz we knew no one but Mrs. Kirby, who had everybody on her mind. She was an institution—you felt she might put you on a list."[10]

Her first words of Georgiana were descriptive of the woman's power and position. Overall, she was respectful and awed by the reformist as an elder woman who shared a similar enthusiasm for cultural pursuits, but who had also experienced the harsher realities of living in an isolated frontier town.

Georgiana had now lived more than a quarter-century in Santa Cruz and was more than a little removed from the early zeal she had possessed when she first donned Turkish pants with the flamboyant Eliza Farnham. There was a cynicism in her attitude that was apparent to the perceptive Mrs. Foote, who was also quick to notice the underlying loneliness. Georgiana's forceful manner and radical viewpoints were a bit frightening, too, for the young woman, and she was therefore quite careful in her straightforward appraisal of the Kirbys.

Mary Hallock Foote's New England background gave her an appreciation and understanding of Georgiana's past that the people of Santa Cruz missed. She was further able to assess Georgiana's Brook Farm experience and its impact upon her life in the passing years. She aptly called it "a slight sickness of the soul,"[11] partly in reference to the reformist's characteristic exasperation with the world around her, but also in recognition of something deeper.

> [Mrs. Kirby] never could forget that once she had wiped dishes with Margaret Fuller and sat on doorsteps on spring nights and talked philosophy with George William Curtis—young, then, and quite godlike in appearance as she described him. The Brook Farm chapter must have been a short one, but it seemed to have altered the values of her whole subsequent existence and given her a slight sickness of the soul. What could come after the intensity of companionships like those! She had gone out to California at a time when every woman had to marry if she expected to live in peace. She would have been one of the plainest, yet she was beset with offers—"and I took the little tanner," she remarked with her usual irreverence and air of detachment. She did well, most persons would have said! They were married on horseback in a brief stop for the purpose in front of a magistrate's office. She had a great sense of story and used her own life as conversational material with a frankness that suggested an equal freedom with another's privacies. She was like Esmond's muse of History, 'familiar but not heroic.'12

Mrs. Foote was able to see that Georgiana had remained altogether passionate in her loyalty to the New England intellectual elite, the source of her inspiration. Contacts with social reformers and literary talents from the East Coast were always exceedingly important to Georgiana, nearly to the point of obsession. In the years after Eliza's departure, Georgiana occasionally refreshed her memories by entertaining the renowned and famous. In 1871, for example, she extended a formal invitation to Ralph Waldo Emerson (who declined), and then in the following season she had received the national suffragist leaders. Georgiana had also served tea to Mark Twain and once rode over the mountain to see her old benefactor, Horace Greeley, on his brief visit to San Jose.

Georgiana seemed to become more preoccupied with the ideas and memories of earlier days as she grew older. She wrote a

piece entitled "My First Visit to Brook Farm," a factual sketch
with fictional characters, which appeared in *Overland Monthly*,
and then composed "Reminiscences of Brook Farm," for *Old and
New*, the publication of the Unitarian Society of New England.
She later commented that she wrote these articles in fear that no
one else would set down their memories of Brook Farm. Her friends
Lorenzo Fowler and Samuel Wells published Georgiana's theory on
heredity entitled *Transmission, or Variation of Character through
the Mother*, in 1877. Her work then began on the autobiographical
Years of Experience, which concentrated solely upon the years
before her arrival in California.

Mary Hallock Foote was sharp in her perception of
Georgiana's motivations, and she applied her critique further with
a literary sketch of the Kirby household. It was plain that she
was never at ease with Georgiana's tendency to hammer her
convictions upon others, or to pry liberally into someone else's
affairs, but she was also impressed with the older woman's
capabilities.

> The Kirbys were called rich; Mr. Kirby was a tanner in
> the days when tanners had their hands and their pits full
> of business, and if they did not make money, they must
> have been exceptionally stupid, which Mr. Kirby was not.
> Still, he was not at all a bookish man nor intellectual in
> his wife's sense of the word. They lived in a large house
> in a garden that filled the whole block. There was
> neither symmetry nor arrangement but much that was
> beautiful and botanical, and it gave you a sense of
> largesse, of crowding, of casting and giving away, in
> keeping with the climate. It had a grape arbor like a
> long green-lighted alley where I used to draw the Kirby
> girls, especially Georgie, who was the prettiest and the
> gentlest.
>
> Mrs. Kirby's life, as she depicted it with her
> extraordinary gift of language, struck me as being
> somewhat like her garden, heterogeneous and crowded,
> yet there was room in it for great loneliness, one surmised.
> She was a difficult woman to be quite just to; she made a
> great appeal to me. Intellectually she was far in advance
> of the town, of any town of those days no older than Santa
> Cruz. Some of her theories that were new at that time

and risky, to say the least (like birth control), she drove
so hard that whoever did not agree with her was quite
likely to hate her. Reformers are seldom tactful and she
was incapable of that wisdom which allows other people
"to be uncomfortable in their own way." She made me at
times excessively uncomfortable, not to say "mad,"
talking to me about my most private affairs with a view
to a sort of enlightenment I should not have dreamed of
asking from her. But when I came to wean my baby the
following spring, she may have saved his life; she was
the first person who taught me to beware of ordinary cow-
stable milk. That was very advanced then. She gave me
a formula for my baby's food which would not disgrace a
baby doctor today.

She took me for many drives (I can't think of any
kindness she did not try to show) along roads she had
galloped over when they were cattle trails, telling me in
her fashion of the monologue the early history of each
home as we passed it. It was the truth as nearly as one
with such a fatal facility in word could be expected to tell
it, and she was bitter-shrewd! The life of the place had
been rather cruel to her. She told me she owned the first
copy of Leaves of Grass that ever came to that coast.
There was one other person in Santa Cruz with whom she
thought she might venture to share it and he was
faithless to her injunction not to pass it on. Her laugh,
when she described the sensation the book made as the
consequence of that indiscretion, was about as cheerful as
a stone dropped into a foot of water in the bottom of a
well.[13]

Georgiana's last years were painful. She developed
arthritis so badly in her hands that a special set of reins was
designed so that she could drive a buggy. And the completion of the
manuscript for *Years of Experience* was an agonizing effort with a
hand-held pen. But worse than the physical trials were the
emotional ones—the death in 1879 of her daughter Georgiana
Bruce, and the death of her youngest child, Phillip, in 1884.

Georgiana herself lingered more than a month with a heart
ailment before she died at the age of 68, on January 27, 1887, shortly
after the release of her autobiography.

Long notices describing the adventures of Georgiana and Eliza Farnham appeared in both the *Santa Cruz Sentinel* and the *San Francisco Chronicle*, and each was generous in its eulogy.

"Mrs. Kirby was a woman who took a deep and earnest interest in all questions that she believed were for the benefit of humanity," said the *Chronicle* writer. "Her mind and character were keenly analytical. She despised all sham and insincerity. She had the rare faculty of entering into the thoughts of others with an intuitive perception, and of sharing their sorrows through her great-hearted sympathy. All up and down this coast are men and women who, when they hear of her death, will remember her as one who aided them in time of trouble. She firmly believed that there is no death to the soul—that death is only a birth into new experience."[14]

She was buried with her children at the Kirby family plot at the Odd Fellows Cemetery in Santa Cruz, following a memorial service at the Unity Church. The sermon was delivered by Mrs. E. L. Watson.[15]

When the women's rights movement began in the nineteenth century, it received nationwide attention from the platform, the pulpit, and the press. But the cause was seldom viewed with objectivity, and its leaders were never granted full credibility. It has taken the contemporary women's rights movement to shed the finer light of understanding on the philosophy and actions of the early feminists and to reveal their struggle as a parallel fight for total equality. Georgiana Bruce Kirby and her friend Eliza Farnham were leaders in the reform movement as it developed in the West, through their thoughts, writings, and actions.

Notes

Years of Experience, 1818–1850

1. Georgiana Bruce Kirby (hereafter GBK), *Years of Experience: An Autobiographical Narrative* (New York: Putnam, 1887) (hereafter YE), p. 2. In YE, GBK left a detailed record of her first thirty-two years. It is upon YE and Helen Giffen's original manuscript and research that this chapter is based.

2. YE, p. 1. Edmund was only the nominal son of Sir Peter Stradwick (sometimes spelled Strudwick). Stradwick's wife, Cabera Desart, had gone with him to Chantilly, where she received the enamored attentions of the Prince of Condé, Louis Joseph. Edmund was born as the illegitimate son of this French baronet, but was reared as the second male offspring of Sir Peter and an heir to the Stradwick estate. Edmund was educated to the life of a gentleman and grew up both in England and France. Susan Stradwick was the child of Edmund's second marriage. She became the beneficiary of his affection and remained his constant companion from the time she left boarding school at the age of seventeen until he died when she was thirty. Together they had enjoyed an extravagant lifestyle that left only a fraction of the estate after Edmund's demise.

3. YE, pp. 4–5.

4. YE, p. 12.

5. YE, p. 29.

6. YE, p. 30.

7. Spencer was married to the daughter of Thomas Elliot, a famous English organmaker.

8. YE, p. 38.

9. YE, pp. 41–42.

10. YE, p. 79.

11. YE, p. 79.

12. YE, p. 81.

13. YE, pp. 82–83.

14. YE, pp. 84–85.

15. YE, pp. 85–86.

16. GBK and Margaret Fuller remained friends until Fuller's death in July, 1850, when she, her husband, and her child drowned off the coast of New York, on returning from Italy.

17. Lane's theory greatly impressed GBK. See Journal, footnote 1.

18. YE, p. 187.

19. Isaac Hecker later converted to Catholocism and founded the order known as the Paulists.

20. YE, p. 190.

21. Eliza Farnham (hereafter EF), *California, In-Doors and Out* (New York: Dix, Edwards & Co., 1856; reprint, Nieuwkoop: De Graaf, 1972, with an introduction by Madeleine B. Stern) (hereafter CIO). For other accounts of EF's life, see Samuel Burhans, Jr., *Burhans Genealogy* (New York: 1894), pp. 180, 193; [Eliza Farnham], *Eliza Woodson; Or, The Early Days of One of the World's Workers* (New York: 1864), a fictional account; "Eliza Wood Burhans Farnham," in *Dictionary of American Biography; Notable American Women, 1607–1950* (Cambridge, Mass.: Harvard University Press, 1971) (hereafter NAW) I, pp. 598-600; and *American Reformers* (New York: H. W. Wilson, 1985), pp. 283-284, and Eliza

Farnham, *Life in Prairie Land* (New York: Harper & Bros., 1846; reprint, Nieuwkoop: De Graaf, 1972, with an introduction by Madeleine B. Stern).

22. W. David Lewis, *From Newgate to Dannemora: The Rise of the Penitentiary in New York, 1796–1848* (Ithaca: Cornell University Press, 1965), pp. 251-256. Estelle B. Freedman, *Their Sisters' Keepers: Women's Prison Reform in America, 1830-1930* (Ann Arbor: University of Michigan Press, 1984), p. 48.

23. YE, p. 218.

24. YE, p. 218.

25. YE, p. 193.

26. *The History of Woman Suffrage,* ed. Elizabeth Cady Stanton, Susan B. Anthony, Matilda Joslyn Gage, *et al.*, 6 vols. (New York: Fowler & Wells, 1881–1886) (hereafter HWS), I, p. 669.

27. Marmaduke B. Sampson was an English phrenologist and London correspondent for the *American Phrenological Journal.* Marmaduke B. Sampson, *Rationale of Crime, And Its Appropriate Treatment; Being a Treatise on Criminal Jurisprudence Considered in Relation to Cerebral Organization;...with Notes and Illustrations by E. W. Farnham* (New York: D. Appleton & Co., 1846.); Madeleine B. Stern, "Mathew B. Brady and the *Rationale of Crime:* A Discovery in Daguerreotypes," *Quarterly Journal of the Library of Congress* (July, 1974), pp. 128-135.

28. YE, p. 224.

29. YE, p. 231.

30. YE, p. 268.

31. YE, p. 314.

32. YE, p. 315.

The People of the Place, 1850–1864

1. Maude Howe [Elliott] and Florence Howe Hall, *Laura Bridgman* (Boston: Little, Brown, and Co., 1903), p. 232; Lewis, pp. 250, 256.

2. Eliza Farnham, *Woman & Her Era* (New York: A. J. Davis, 1864).

3. During his visits to the California Territory, Farnham had quickly allied himself with the Yankee point-of-view. When Isaac Graham and other local "foreigners" were arrested and sent to Mexico in 1841, Farnham followed. He eventually engineered both release and compensation for the frontiersman. In later writings, Farnham portrayed Graham as a "stout, sturdy backwoodsman," a heroic example of American enterprise in opposition to the culture of the native Californio. In return, Graham helped the lawyer secure land near his own. Recorded deeds show that Thomas Farnham obtained title in August, 1847, to land purchased at $1 per acre from eleven men, all native Indians, who "affixed the sign of the Holy Cross," to acknowledge sale of the property north and northwest of Mission Santa Cruz. The name "Rancho La Libertad" (Spanish for liberty) was ironic.

4. CIO, xiv-xv; *Eliza Farnham's Bride-Ship: An 1849 Circular Inviting Young Women of the East to Go to California* (The Book Club of San Francisco, 1952.)

5. Catharine M. Sedgwick, *Life and Letters* (New York: Harper & Bros., 1871), p. 312.

6. *Alta California*, June 7, 1849.

7. *Alta California*, June 10, 1849.

8. CIO, p. 22.

9. CIO, p. 24.

10. CIO, p. 41.

11. One of Mrs. Farnham's first and most lasting friendships in Santa Cruz was with a man whose character and style was as peculiar in its

own way as her own. This was Isaac Graham, the frontiersman who Thomas Farnham had rescued years before. In her writings, Eliza details her varied encounters with Mr. Graham and recounts some of the escapades in his life—the murder of his wife's brother by his own son from another marriage, for example. In a description of his appearance, she said that Graham "with his rifle at his back, and shoes down at heel, presented in his exterior a curious mixture of the hunter and the man of leisure." CIO, p. 49.

12. CIO, pp. 42–43.

13. CIO, pp. 86-87.

14. EF to Fowler and Wells, Santa Cruz, November 15, 1850, reprinted in Madeleine B. Stern, "Two Letters from the Sophisticates of Santa Cruz," *The Book Club of California Quarterly News-Letter* (Summer, 1968), 33(3): p. 55.

15. CIO, p. 181.

16. CIO, p. 136.

17. CIO, pp. 154–155.

18. CIO, p. 155.

19. CIO, pp. 156–157.

20. CIO, pp. 164–165.

21. CIO, p. 166.

22. CIO, p. 107.

23. GBK to Charlotte Fowler Wells, Santa Cruz, 1851? reprinted in Madeleine B. Stern, "Two Letters from the Sophisticates of Santa Cruz," *The Book Club of California Quarterly News-Letter* (Summer, 1968), 33(3): pp. 59–60 (hereafter TL) The originals are in the Fowler-Wells Collections, Collection of Regional History and Archives, Cornell University. The two Fowler brothers lectured throughout the country and tested their ideas on phrenology on the most famous citizens of the day. A cast of Eliza's head was kept in their office, and Lorenzo Fowler judged that she "comprehends

principles far beyond the common mind; has self-directing talents; disposed to lead and influence others; crown of the head large, joined with uncommon energy and stability of purpose. Friendship is very strong, but love is platonic. The head is masculine...." TL, p. 52. Later, when she returned to New York after her stay in California, another analysis by the Fowler brothers revealed that Eliza's head "is more largely developed through the middle and back portions, indicating more stoutness of character, more of the heroic, earnest, and efficient, and more breadth of affection" than the average. TL, p. 61.

24. TL, p. 60. On May 30, 1868, the *Santa Cruz Sentinel* published a notice about the demolition of Eliza's house: "An Old Landmark Gone—The old and singularly shaped house, above and fronting on the potrero, built many years ago (but never finished) by Mrs. Farnham, has been torn down to be replaced by a new farm house. The former building had five gables and was a wild looking edifice. Its dormer windows strangely contrasted with the beautiful fields and romantic scenery surrounding it."

25. TL, p. 56.

26. TL, p. 56.

27. Leon Rowland, *Santa Cruz: The Early Years: The Collected Historical Writings of Leon Rowland* (Santa Cruz: Paper Vision Press, 1980), p. 141.

28. See Journal entry, December 14, 1852.

29. See Journal entry, December 14, 1852.

30. See Journal entry, January 25, 1854.

31. *Santa Cruz Sentinel*, July 5, 1856, p. 2.

32. Eliza Farnham, *Woman & Her Era* (New York: A. J. Davis, 1864).

33. HWS, I, p. 669.

34. NAW, I, p. 598.

35. *Santa Cruz Sentinel*, June 2, 1866

36. HWS, III, p. 765.

37. Helen Hunt Jackson, *Bits of Travel at Home* (Boston: Roberts Bros., 1880.)

III. Muse of Santa Cruz, 1865–1887

1. *Santa Cruz Sentinel*, August 26, 1871, p. 2.

2. *Santa Cruz Sentinel*, August 5, 1871, p. 3.

3. *Santa Cruz Sentinel*, August 12, 1871, p. 3.

4. *Watsonville Pajaronian*, August 10, 1871, p. 2.

5. *Santa Cruz Sentinel*, August 26, 1871, p. 2.

6. *Santa Cruz Sentinel*, August 26, 1871, p. 2.

7. *Santa Cruz Sentinel*, September 30, 1871, p. 2.

8. *Santa Cruz Sentinel*, March 30, 1872, p. 3.

9. *Santa Cruz Sentinel*, March 30, 1872, p. 3.

10. Mary Hollock Foote, *A Victorian Gentlewoman in the Far West: The Reminiscences of Mary Hallock Foote*, edited with an introduction by Rodman W. Paul (San Marino, Calif.: The Huntington Library, 1972) (hereafter VGW), p. 141. A fictionalized account of Foote's Santa Cruz sojourn, including a characterization of GBK named Mrs. Elliott, is contained in Wallace Stegner's novel, *Angle of Repose* (New York: Doubleday, 1971).

11. VGW, p. 144.

12. VGW, p. 144.

13. VGW, pp. 142–143.

14. *Santa Cruz Sentinel*, January 29, 1887, p. 3.

15. *Santa Cruz Sentinel*, February 1, 1887, p. 2.

GEORGIANA BRUCE KIRBY.

Georgiana Bruce Kirby. From Ella Sterling Cummins, *The Story of the Files: A Review of Californian Writers and Literature* (San Francisco, 1893) p. 162.

Georgiana Bruce Kirby. *(Courtesy Society of California Pioneers, San Francisco)*

Eliza Wood Burhans Farnham. From Samuel Burhans, Jr., *Burhans Genealogy* (New York: 1894).

SHIP ANGELIQUE.

CALIFORNIA ASSOCIATION OF AMERICAN WOMEN.

NEW YORK. February 2d, 1849.

The death of my husband, Thomas J. Farnham, Esq., at San Francisco, in September last. renders it expedient that I should visit California during the coming season. Having a desire to accomplish some greater good by my journey thither than to give the necessary attention to my private affairs, and believing that the presence of women would be one of the surest checks upon many of the evils that are apprehended there, I desire to ask attention to the following sketch of a plan for organizing a party of such persons to emigrate to that country.

Among the many privations and deteriorating influences to which the thousands who are flocking thither will be subjected, one of the greatest is the absence of woman, with all her kindly cares and powers, so peculiarly conservative to man under such circumstances.

It would exceed the limits of this circular to hint at the benefits that would flow to the growing population of that wonderful region, from the introduction among them of intelligent, virtuous and efficient women. Of such only, it is proposed to make up this company. It is believed that there are hundreds, if not thousands, of such females in our country who are not bound by any tie that would hold them here, who might, by going thither. have the satisfaction of employing themselves greatly to the benefit and advantage of those who are there, and at the same time of serving their own interest more effectually than by following any employment that offers to them here.

It is proposed that the company shall consist of persons not under twenty-five years of age. who shall bring from their clergyman, or some authority of the town where they reside, satisfactory testimonials of education. character. capacity, &c., and who can contribute the sum of two hundred and fifty dollars, to defray the expenses of the voyage. make suitable provision for their accommodation after reaching San Francisco, until they shall be able to enter upon some occupation for their support. and create a fund to be held in reserve for the relief of any who may be ill, or otherwise need aid before they are able to provide for themselves.

It is believed that such an arrangement, with one hundred or one hundred and thirty persons. would enable the company to purchase or charter a vessel, and fit it up with every thing necessary to comfort on the voyage. and that the combination of all for the support of each, would give such security, both as to health, person and character. as would remove all reasonable hesitation from the minds of those who may be disposed and able to join such a mission. It is intended that the party shall include six or eight respectable married men and their families.

Those who desire further information will receive it by calling on the subscriber at

ELIZA W FARNHAM.

The New-York built Packet Ship Angelique has been engaged to take out this Association. She is a spacious vessel. fitted up with state rooms throughout and berths of good size, well ventilated and provided in every way to secure a safe. speedy and comfortable voyage. She will be ready to sail from New-York about the 12th or 15th of April

We, the undersigned, having been made acquainted with the plan proposed by Mrs. Farnham, in the above circular, hereby express our approbation of the same, and recommend her to those who may be disposed to unite with her in it. as worthy the trust and confidence necessary to its successful conduct.

Hon. J. W. EDMONDS, Judge Superior Court
Hon. W. T. McCOUN, Late Vice Chancellor.
Hon. B. F. BUTLER, Late U. S. Attorney.
Hon. H. GREELEY.
ISAAC T. HOPPER, Esq.
FREEMAN HUNT, Esq.
THOMAS C. DOREMUS, Esq.

W. C. BRYANT, Esq.
SHEPHERD KNAPP, Esq.
Rev. GEORGE POTTS. D. D.
Rev. HENRY WARD BEECHER.
Miss CATHARINE M. SEDGWICK.
Mrs. C. M. KIRKLAND

NESBITT. PRINTER.

"California Association of American Women," Eliza Farnham's Brideship Circular. (Courtesy California Historical Society, San Francisco)

Richard Kirby. *(Courtesy California Historical Society, San Francisco)*

Kirby Homestead, Rancho La Salud. (*Courtesy* California Historical Society, San Francisco)

Village of Santa Cruz. (Courtesy Special Collections, University Library, University of California, Santa Cruz)

Residence of R. C. Kirby. From *Santa Cruz County, California* (San Francisco: Wallace W. Elliott & Co., 1879).

R. C. Kirby's Tannery. From *Santa Cruz County, California* (San Francisco: Wallace W. Elliott & Co., 1879).

SANTA CRUZ AMERICANA.

"Santa Cruz Americana," by Mary Hallock Foote, from "A Sea-Port on the Pacific," *Scribner's Monthly* , 16 (August 1878), p. 456. "[The garden] had a grape arbor like a long, green-lighted alley, where I used to draw the Kirby girls, especially Georgie, who was the prettiest and the gentlest." From M. H. Foote, *A Victorian Gentlewoman in the Far West* (San Marino, Calif.: The Huntington Library, 1972), p. 142

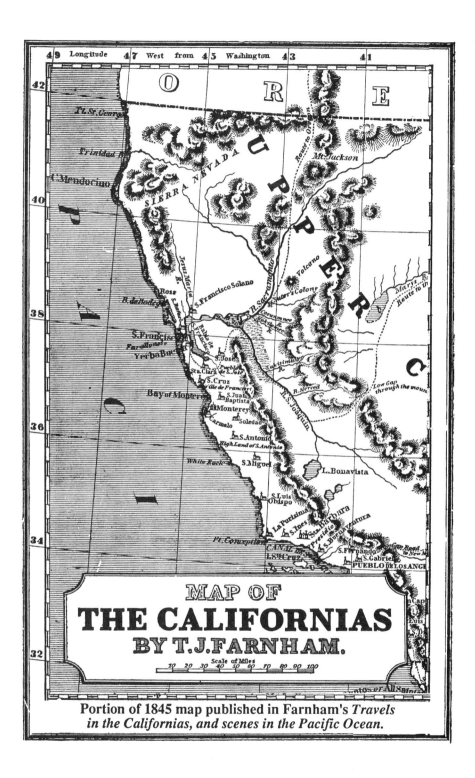

MAP OF
THE CALIFORNIAS
BY T.J.FARNHAM.

Scale of Miles
10 20 30 40 50 60 70 80 90 100

Portion of 1845 map published in Farnham's *Travels
in the Californias, and scenes in the Pacific Ocean.*

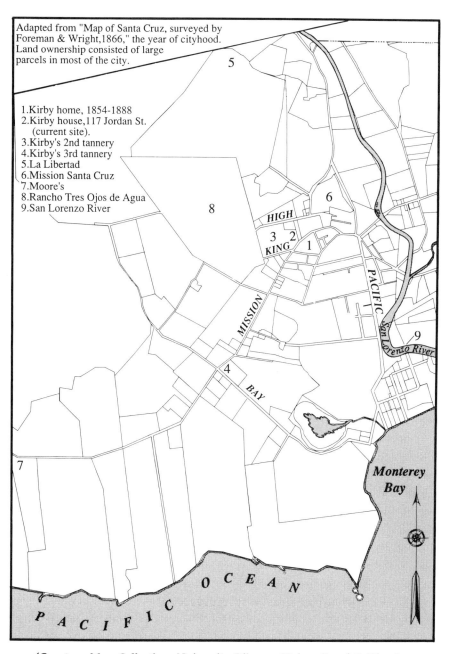

Adapted from "Map of Santa Cruz, surveyed by
Foreman & Wright,1866," the year of cityhood.
Land ownership consisted of large
parcels in most of the city.

5

1. Kirby home, 1854-1888
2. Kirby house,117 Jordan St.
   (current site).
3. Kirby's 2nd tannery
4. Kirby's 3rd tannery
5. La Libertad
6. Mission Santa Cruz
7. Moore's
8. Rancho Tres Ojos de Agua
9. San Lorenzo River

6

8

HIGH

3 2
KING 1

PACIFIC

San Lorenzo River

9

MISSION

4

BAY

7

Monterey
Bay

PACIFIC OCEAN

(*Courtesy Map Collection, University Library, University of California,
Santa Cruz*)

The Journal of
Georgiana Bruce Kirby

Das Tagebuch

December 14, 1852–January 26, 1860

Santa Cruz, California

The Journal of Georgiana Bruce Kirby
1852–1860

Dec. 14, 1852

The day is blustering and rainy and cold, but I feel in better health and spirits, especially the latter, than for some time. This morning immediately after breakfast I rode my good old Rosea over into the "off hollow" and onto the hills beyond, wishing to see where "Tom" had hauled the new fencing stuff. It always puts me in good spirits to gallop up the hills and view the wild mountain scenery, so on my return, after taking in the clothes and all the wood that was chopped, as the clouds looked ominous, I concluded that today for the first time in my life I would commence a journal. I think that perhaps I may die and my babe live, in which case it would be pleasant for the latter to have some record of my external and spiritual life during these important months; or should I survive this great trial of my physical powers and live to see my child grow up, it will be interesting to me to see how far and in what manner my present and succeeding states of mind may have had influence in forming the character and consequently the external appearance of my child.[1]

Since I was a girl of eighteen I have been ever conscious of the most intense desire to become a mother. The thought (in anticipation) of the condition in which I now find myself used to fill my whole being with joy. Often and often when alone with nature my soul had been lifted up as it were to higher spheres and so filled with a sense of harmony and melody that I was obliged to relieve myself by a long recitative, not, owing to my inferior vocal

organs, at all worthy of the emotions that gave rise to it. It is not
that I am especially fond of little babies, for I am not, though I
doubt not that this instinct will in due time become developed in
me; but I do earnestly love to watch the unfolding of character and
intellect. I love so much to influence youth aright—to arouse moral
ambition, to instil by precept and example a thorough respect for
labor and, oh, that my own child, be it boy or girl, may have some
monumental noble trait—some beautiful spiritual gift, like music,
for instance, and no mean streak or fatal weakness. I desire that my
child have a generous nature, good common sense, and industry, at
the very least. My husband has so many excellent qualities that I
am deficient in, and also so excellent a temperament that, unless
other causes have force enough to counteract the good, I feel we
have every reason to hope for the best.

     For more than two months I have been suffering from the
ordinary ailments of such a condition and they are such as do not
conduce to healthy intellectual action by any means. Mr. K[irby],
kind, active, and ever cheerful, gets up and prepares breakfast,
brings me chocolate and toast or whatnot to bed—kills and dresses a
chicken for my dinner or saddles the horse for me to take a short
ride—then hurries off to the tan yard (two miles or so).[2] At night
he often goes to the mission after closing work and is then sure to
bring home a variety of articles with which to tempt my appetite
or in some way contribute to my comfort.[3] Our rancho with its
hollows and gulches and noble sweep of hills exactly suits me, but I
have been used to mixing in pretty large circles and miss the
pleasant and healthy excitement caused by the friction of mind on
mind. I long for flowers and fruits and music, too, but one cannot
expect every good in the present state of society and I have many as
it is—unsurpassed beauty of scenery and climate, good health,
neither poverty or riches, and the most devoted friend in my
husband. The other day Mr. K. brought home a balm of Gilead tree
about 4 1/2 feet high and planted it just opposite the kitchen
window. It really gladdened by heart as I watched it constantly
during the day as I would a child. It was the first step in the way
of *refined* cultivation and gives me faith in the future roses, lilies,
dahlias, and so forth, gives me faith that I shall one day gather
glorious red currants and Antwerp raspberries and luscious English
gooseberries in our own garden on our own Rancho La Salud, near

Santa Cruz, California.

The day before yesterday (Sunday) we went to see Mr. and Mrs. Sawin who live "up the coast" maybe two miles from the mission.[4] Owing to the first rains which lasted pretty much for three weeks and to K. being so busy that he had to raise sheds and stables on Sunday instead of taking me on a *pasear,*[5] for more than three months previous to this I had not been off the rancho or seen a woman and the Sawins are so friendly that I enjoyed this visit very much. It is three miles from here to the mission and those women who have side saddles and horses at command are yet so occupied by their housekeeping cares that they are unable, excepting at distant intervals, to leave home for a day. There are no sisters or aunts or grown-up daughters to take their places while absent and if it should happen, which it has not as yet among any other class than the roughest mission [illegible], that any such sisters, aunts, or grown-up daughters did exist, then before you could turn around they would be certainly snatched up and themselves immediately in the same plight as the rest of the women and quite as badly off as before. When I came down here a little more than two years ago, there were but few families and those of the roughest sort. The Imuses, Hecoxes, Bennetts, Hollenbecks, Anthonys, Moores, and such as had not parted with their neat Yankee habits in housekeeping, the Sawins, Meaders, Cases, there was no person with the exception of Mrs. Sawin whose manners and habits of living approaches the lady-like. The Meaders are Mormons and I like both father, mother, and daughter exceedingly. They are very genuine, very sincere, very clean, with a large stock of common sense and kindliness. "Mother Case," who is also Mr. Case so far as ruling goes, is a very pious, gossiping old lady who sets the best table of any one in Santa Cruz as yet. They have been here many years and are well stocked with daily comforts.[6]

At the time I have alluded to there were scarcely any buildings in the mission but the old adobe ones, no fences up the coast or down, with the exception of a bit of Spanish fencing by Rodriguez or Majors which had to be rebuilt every year.[7] Now from the mission fully up to Moore's the land is taken up and fenced well as a general thing. Several families raise a variety of vegetables, but as yet no orchard or nursery has been planted in this region, and there is no wild fruit but the strawberries twelve miles up the coast. The pears in the mission orchard are tasteless things and the apples from San Juan [Bautista] a slight improvement on the crab and yet this will one day be the finest fruit region in California.

In coming to Santa Cruz it was my intention to teach school. There were many girls belonging to these western families of sufficient promise to interest me in them. I could and desired to not only instruct them in books but in their personal habits of cleanliness, neatness, order, courtesy, how to make and mend clothes and so forth; but the pious young villain who was then keeping the mixed school, one of the cloth who frequently exhorted in the meeting (Methodist), reigned supreme. The regular local minister, Mr. Brier, a self-conceited, bawling brute, without a spark of tenderness, used all his influence against me in this, and, added to the unpopularity of Mrs. Farnham, at whose house I was staying, rendered the entire plan abortive.[8] This teacher afterward seduced some of the young girls and had to leave in the night—went on to the boards in San Francisco and afterwards joined the filibustering expedition to the Sandwich Islands.[9] After giving up the school I took to gardening, much to the benefit of my health and improvement of my pocket. The soil proved too sandy for onions. Russell, Mrs. F's farmer, who had induced me to leave San F. by a series of lies about Mrs. Farnham's wealth and what she would give me, failed afterward to help me in any gardening as he promised.[10] He managed so badly that after dropping 10 acres of potatoes the estate was so much in debt that I could not ask for the one I was to have. For more than a year I did not make one cent. Then I went down with Bryant Hill to the Pajaro Valley to cook for his men.[11] He was the first American that settled there and I remained there six months in a house without a chair or bedstead or table (with the exception of the boards on tressels that we and the men ate off). For three months we had no windows, the light came through the door which was left open, no looking glass, no flat irons. I ironed the bosom and collars of two white shirts with a half-pint, tin tumbler kept constantly half full of boiling water. I worked very hard indeed. My only comfort was a game of whist after eight o'clock with Mrs. Thrift, a young New England woman who had married an illiterate young Southerner, who I had with me. She was avowedly an abolitionist and I respected her for this and hoped to find in her a companion and friend, but I found her selfish in the extreme, without a shadow of aspiration, self-willed and wholly wanting in the common traits of New England women—judgement, skill in the various domestic departments, economy and so forth. I was very sorry to give her up but she obliged me to.

I had grown old in fretting about Mrs. Farnham's troubles and perplexities. She was so ignorant of business, so careless, so easily imposed on, and at the same time so determined to get so much under weigh at once that she was constantly in debt or in hot water somehow. She let Buckle, who had $7,000 of her husband's money, persuade her to set up farming without any title.[12] He presently failed—she took Russell, an Irishman without self-respect, without system, without knowledge of how to treat or deal with men and with no idea of straight-forwardness, of speaking the truth—simply a skillful and industrious worker, and trusted to him management of her farm in Santa Cruz. After that she took a half-fool, half-knave (Pelton) who did no better.[13] Then she married the greatest blackguard in the country who strikes and otherwise ill treats her.[14] At the time I write she has returned to him for the second time. Her children are tossed about here and there and her property wholly unattended to and unproductive.

Dec. 15th: Last night there was ice on the pools a quarter of an inch thick and about 10 a. m. there was quite a brisk shower of snow, which lasted some five minutes and then changed to rain. I believe myself incapable of experiencing pleasure excepting through association. So this snow reminding me of happy days in Canada and Massachusetts fairly made my heart merry. Last evening I was reading the closing scene in Browning's *Paracelsus*; what wonderful power and yet what fineness, what delicacy in this man's experiences.[15] Somehow I was led to compare the philosophy of Paracelsus with that of the manly James, especially in their enlightened acceptance of the past—their just interpretation of it as the necessary prelude to the future.[16] I have the most intimate sympathy with the views advanced by Henry James. The subjects being so comprehensive are necessarily treated very imperfectly, but still what he gives you is clear, sound wheat, fit to be assimilated with the inmost of the blood. How heartily I agree with him in his contempt for the teachings of the modern church, mean, cringing, self-blaspheming. I am happy in remembering that notwithstanding the soul-searching religious experience I went through in my youth—lasting indeed through years, I never for one moment believed that God regarded me in any other light than a friendly one. I never knew what remorse meant. I never believed that God would bless me for Christ's sake, for I felt intuitively that our primal relation was a good, harmonious one. I never would thank him for goods enjoyed which were withheld from others. To entertain any of these sentiments struck me as degrading the character of the deity below that of inferior men. With what, for a child, were superhuman efforts I made confession of stealing plums from a dish, a humming top from a shop, and of sundry less heinous crimes, feeling that in doing so I must resign all hopes of the world's respect, but I knew no other emotions than courage, love of truth, desire to stand honestly with myself. I had much reverence, much love of being loved, steady aspiration after inmost truths. How could I with my very moderate intellectual powers build a harmonious system out of the savage discordant materials around me? I was interested always in theological questions and yet theology would by no means cling to me, God be thanked, for it was all false and would have made me less loving and less intelligent than I am. Channing's mild moralities, Carlyle's indignant ravings, Parker's bold analysis of the the religious sentiments, dreams of the immediate perfection of society by association, satisfactory working at "fragmentary" reforms, now James puts the keystone on, which authenticates all of these.[17]

Dec. 22nd: The rain of ten days and nights and the winds that sent seven vessels on shore have at length, so appearances would agree, passed away. The earth is green, the sky fair. Bryant Hill, who had $25,000 worth of produce on board two of the vessels and who supposes his rancho, with $25,000 worth more in bags and heaps of potatoes undug, is for the most part under water and the house blown into the river, left here to return this morning. He came up with his two partners a week ago and owing to the rise in the San Lorenzo and the Soquel Creek he could not cross to return. I pray that his affairs be not so desperate as he apprehends, for I long to see Eleanor and the child and she must be so very weary of waiting to join him. I wish also that he may keep the 2,000 acres in the Pajaro that so satisfy his farming aspirations.

I am out of reading matter and have neither the health or energy to attempt to study as means of occupying my time and mind. Once in two weeks the mail brings the *Tribune, A. S. Standard,* and *Freeman.*[18] When these are read, first hurriedly and then carefully, I am in the same condition as before. The last *Tribune* contained Parker's discourse on Webster. It is a just verdict to which the future will attest. I am glad these three unworthy idols of the American people, Clay, Calhoun, and Webster, are dead. It may be that better men will gradually fill their places in the public estimation. When I think of Mann, Sumner, Giddings, Phillips, and Garrison I agree with Dickens, "That if this were a Republic of intellect and worth, instead of vaporing and jobbing, they would not want the lever to keep it in motion," but the great mass of people in all classes are so wholly wanting in integrity of character, are so shallow and at the same time so self-conceited, that one is almost tempted to despair of their ever making radical progress towards the really good and noble.[19] Whenever any crisis comes to try their metal you hear the ring of tin and brass, nothing better. The nation has no great heart as the German or English people, material gain is its sole object. As a people they have no sentiment, nothing that makes it impossible for them to do the meanest or wickedest thing conceivable.

Janu. 7th, 1853: The remnants of this remarkable rain storm still hang about us. There cannot have been less than 2 1/2 feet of water fallen during these last six weeks. Farming operations are thus put back—no ploughing done as yet. In former years wheat was sowed in November and December. The upper country must be flooded and all planting necessarily stopped for the present. There must be great suffering in the mines. Provisions, especially the staples, flour and pork, were so high that traders waited for a fall before purchasing their winter stock and now the long rain has cut off communication. A few speculators buy up all the flour and pork and hold it at $35.00 and $40.00 and $47.00 the barrel. If the railroad were built between California and Missouri it would equalize the market. The rich valleys on the route would help to supply this land of non-producers. Potatoes have risen to 8¢ and ere long will be 10¢ the lb I doubt not, so what Bryant H. loses by the rot and extra freight will be made up.

I have just mailed long letters to the good Robert Purvis, Rebecca Plumly, George Bradford, Moses Atwood, and others.[20] This work occupied all my well hours for nearly two weeks. I enjoy myself very little owing to this inveterate dyspepsia. Two weeks ago tonight John Bowman, a Quaker farmer from Byberry, Pa., arrived.[21] He had been detained a week in the Santa Clara valley by the rain and had a great time crossing the mountains. It was well that he had a cheerful heart and a good horse or it might have fared worse with him. He was soaking wet and mud to his knees when he reached here, but in fine spirits, as if he had got home at last. He had spent his last month in Pa., at the house of my beloved friend, Robert Purvis, and brought me letters, "Uncle Tom," and a beautiful daguerreotype of our sweet young friend Tacie Townsend.[22] John Bowman had lived some twenty years in Byberry and I was glad to hear all the news, though I thought it an uncommonly stupid place the 10 months I spent there. R. Purvis is the beautiful star that gives the place any character at all and there are a few pretty fair women, but all hampered by their miserly dolts of fathers or their poverty. The second day of Mr. Bowman's visit was devoted to the gossip of his neighborhood. Mr. B. married a daughter of the high priest in Quakerdom, John Comly. The daughter loved her father best and in business relations sided with him to the great grief and perplexity of her good-natured husband. His wife's relations treated him very meanly and I'm glad he has come out here where his industry, strength, and skill will, in a few years, secure him an independent fortune. His nasal tones and too great enthusiasm at first made me very nervous and irritable, but before he left on Sunday to fetch his trunk and so forth from San F. I had become used to his voice and ways and was really glad to look forward to his return. He will plant the first nursery in Santa Cruz on our land and, besides, make us a garden. After March he will work in the tan yard and may live with us many years. When Mr. K. returned from escorting him by a nearer road to Majors's Rancho, at the foot of the mountains (he goes to San F. to fetch his things), he brought with him some young pine trees and set them around the house. The cattle nibble them and rub against their slender stems. It's such a pity.

It is so delightful here when the rain does stop; we have the most glorious summer weather at once. The birds sing, the Bay is covered with a haze of glory, the earth green as emerald.

Jan. 12th: My health begins to mend. My mind returns to its old picture-making, conversation-holding (imaginary) habits. I regret that I find the exertion of walking disagreeably fatiguing. The various forms of measure (rhythm) that so constantly used to repeat themselves in my mind come back again, also the same vivid conceptions of persons and events as I lie awake at night. Occasionally, too, I have a beautiful dream of being indeed asleep, and the spirit leaving the body finds itself overlooking a noble city, examining its architecture, plan and so forth, it being cold and solemn and clear at night. Oh, that my best dream nights may be reproduced. I have nearly done what sewing I have to do. Next week I shall help them cut potatoes for planting and hope to be strong enough to drop for a few days. Such work seems more at work, more productive than puttering in the house. Tom is ploughing with Barney and Sandy. Mr. Bowman not yet returned. The weather is very squally, at night the vessels are wise enough to run over to Monterey before the rain begins. Freight to San Francisco $20.00 a ton. No flour in the mission for three weeks. Daubenbiss' dam was so deranged by the flood that it has to be repaired.[23] It is $35 and $40 a barrel in San Francisco, and few can afford that price and pay freight ($3. bl) down. We hear of miners at the nearest mining region, back of Sacramento, eating barley at $1.00 the lb and of those who were packing provisions on their backs from the city being frozen to death. As yet no news from the more distant settlements.

Jan. 17th: Three days ago a young friend from Fairfield Co., Pa., by name Albert Brown, passed the night with us.[24] He, with hundreds of others, was driven from the mines by the snow and want of provisions. He had a brother of seventeen with him. He is only nineteen himself, but possesses the energy, firmness, and self-respect of a much older person. He very wisely considered that he would be more likely to obtain work in the country than in the crowd at San F. and so walked to San Jose and across the mountains. He has engaged with Meader for $60 a month and will send for his brother who will also readily find employment, as the fine weather lasts and the farmers are in a hurry to get their crops in. I know not how it is but Tom annoys me more and more by his way of talking. He is very ignorant and has a blustering way of delivering himself, always laughing with a coarse common laugh and emphasis on every sentence with "I'm bothered," "The beggar of a horse," or "beggar of a thing." It is no matter who is talking—how calmly or sensibly and not, of course, directing their conversation to him, he must always join in with his giggle and common-places and vulgarisms as if he were as well informed as any one. It annoys me more than I could wish. I dread the presence of such a person and this dislike seems to accumulate upon itself. Presently there will come a crisis and then I may tolerate him better. He is to cultivate the land for one-third the crop and so will be with us till spring. I do hope we can build a kitchen in which the men can have their meals and sit, and we can have quiet home times in the dining room. I have been reading the Atkinson and Martineau book and find it very suggestive and consoling just as James is.[25] Works based on false sentiment, the outgrowth of a false morality, unless indeed they have the direct power to help renovate society, as "Uncle Tom," are very stupid things. One thing constantly forces itself on the free soul—the danger attending through freedom of speech or action. One does not wish to die and to a well balanced mind the love of their fellows is necessary if one is faithful to one's convictions of what is right. You are not only an outlaw yourself but you involve the well-being of those of your friends who may not be so well able to cope with the difficulties as yourself.

I am in better health from taking arsenic, still the least indiscretion with regard to the nature of my food causes wearisome relapses. To be occupied solely with the sense of pain in the stomach is such sad waste of time and I am so desirous of being cheerful and thoughtful. Mr. Bowman has brought down a few strawberry roots—asparagus and so forth, and one little peach tree. I wish he were more quiet and had some sufficient satisfaction with his own labors, great and small, so as to avoid the necessity of telling of every little thing he does and every movement he makes. It detracts so much from a man's manliness, the constantly asking the suffrages of his fellows. He talks and explains in one endless, nasal monotone and with the most tedious prolixity about all sorts of unimportant and commonplace things, never seeming to think that the people he is talking to be as well informed on the subject as himself, or that the trifling incidents he so minutely describes may be thoroughly uninteresting to his auditors, who for civility sake are obliged to listen against their will and respond occasionally. It is a thousand pities that no one warned him of the disagreeable habit when he was a young man; it serves to alienate many who would otherwise be his warm friends, I doubt not. By talking one-quarter as much he would have twenty times the influence.

Jan. 27th: We planted our first potatoes on the 25th. There was so great a press of work (as is usually the case in a Cal. spring) that I volunteered to drop potatoes. I was so anxious to have Mr. Bowman go on with the garden fence. The first day I got along pretty well, but yesterday at noon I completely gave out and went straight to bed dreading a miscarriage after all I had endured for the sake of a future blessing. Today I am rested somewhat but do not like the symptoms at all—regret that I have no arnica to take. Sent off letters to Tacie, Mother, and Paulina Wright, asking particulars about the new association at Raritan Bay, N. J., in which I am interested.[26] Today it rains a little with a prospect of more behind. It is good for our up-hill barley, only I pray that it stop in reasonable time.

Feb 1st: The weather continues fair and mild. Farming proceeding briskly. I am still very unwell, consumed by "heart-burn," so-called. My work is a burden to me and the constant pain and consequent weakness keeps my mind heavy. I suffer intolerably from thirst and avoid drinking until my tongue is parched, because the liquid increases the heart-burn. Am writing to Phebe Preston of Lancaster Co., Pa., who wrote me lately enclosing a letter from Hanna Mary Bernard, now a student at Oberlin. I have seen the face of but one woman (Mrs. Sawin) in four months and a half and it is likely to be two more before any one will have time to visit. No bright or beautiful thoughts and at the same time no fretfulness or anxiety. K. is so thoroughly kind that he has a tranquilizing effect on me, who am, as a general thing, inclined to be apprehensive of evil and too sensitive to the influence of others.

Feb. 3rd: Sowing barley below the road. Bryant staid over night with us, in fine spirits because of the calmness of the weather which enables him to get off all his produce from Castro's.[27] It is well that he has an excess of hope in his composition, for he has had enough trouble to crush an ordinary person. Success makes such a difference, too, in his looks—when under the influence of hope he is handsome; when oppressed with care, decidedly homely.

I am not sure that anything whatever could relieve or comfort me under my present very depressing condition of health, but if anything could it would be a congenial female companion with whom I could chat and be merry—sympathize and advise.[28] The being alone all day from eight in the morning to seven at night ensures a too great seriousness. There is nothing to call out any other faculties of the mind, fancy, imagination, affection, mirthfulness, nothing in fact to kindle or excite a worthy spirit life. I regret this more than I can express, dreading the effect on the little one. Every good woman needs a companion of her own sex, no matter how numerous or valuable her male acquaintances, no matter how close the union between herself and husband; if she have a genial, loving nature, the want of a female friend is felt as a sad void. I have a fixed habit also of living nearly altogether in the future. Not that I am in the least discontented with my present circumstances; it is a habit that, if I remember rightly, grew out of my desire for knowledge when a young girl. I always hoped something would "happen" in a few years to enable me to attain the intellectual culture I so earnestly desired and which I found myself entirely unable in my cramped circumstances to arrive at. Benevolence and affection always came in to interfere with the fulfillment of aspiration and so the years wore away in ceaseless yearning and the habit became fixed of looking far, far away even to the future of death when social duties and individual aspirations would never conflict. For my life, take it all together and considering my natural tendencies, has been one of severe struggle and suffering, only alleviated by the love I found myself able to attract and the sense of power over growing minds. It would be more desirable for me at this time to take a hearty interest in my housekeeping, but I never did feel the slightest in such things and the cooking is most distasteful and irksome to me. All that I do is done of outward necessity and because there would be a worse state of confusion were it left undone. Then being cut off from society out of my natural sphere, since I cannot exert my natural influence and receive those necessary to me in return, I fail in earnestness, concentrativeness, active internal power. If I had a nice friend with me it would recall me from my vague dreaming to the worth of the actual present. It is folly in moral philosophers to talk absolutely about persons making their own circumstances. It is utterly impossible for me to cause a state of mind in myself which would naturally result from the conflict in other minds. I never *think.* All the nobler intellectual faculties lie dormant.

Wednesday, Feb. 9th: Fine weather still lasts. I rode to the mission last Sunday, took tea at the Whitings' and then went to pass the night at Mrs. Dryden's, the wife of the Methodist Minister.[29] She is in the like case with myself and as her husband was in San F. we slept together and had quite a cheerful time of it. The next day I saw at her house one or two other pleasant women and Mrs. W. is to come up this evening to pass a few days with me. I enjoyed the visit exceedingly and feel better in consequence. On the 6th, sowed cauliflower, asparagus, rhubarb, and onions and set out the strawberry plants.

Feb. 13th: Sowed celery, sea kale and set out the first little peach tree up by the house and the rose bushes around.

I am better—had two days' visit from Mrs. Whiting which has quite made me forget myself and my ailments. She also is to become a mother, so are many other women in the mission, and for the first time after being married many years. The place has become proverbial for its fruitfulness. We are all in a state of partial anxiety about doctors and nurses, those here of the former class being bunglers, giving calomel to a confined woman and losing healthy patients frequently, and most of the latter being filled more or less with old women's superstitions as regards the treatment of new-born babies.

I am reading "Reveries of a Bachelor" to Mr. K. It is good to read just enough to stimulate thought.[30]

Feb. 23rd: Last night the much needed rain came. Tom had given up further ploughing for want of it only yesterday. It is a gentle and not cold rain. They have finished this side of the garden fence and today make a large gate in the place of bars. Last week the mare foaled—I am sorry it is not a horse colt. I am very busy sewing sacs and skirts and so forth. The transplanted rose bushes are putting out their leaves and the rhubarb is getting quite green. Health pretty good, cheerful, busy, very practical, no reading. Two months is a long time to wait the answer to a letter. If there were a weekly mail from the east it would help the matter.

27th: Mr. K. wanted sweet potatoes in the garden. Mr. B. had planted half the sack three weeks or a month ago. Today they fixed the spring with a box and pipes and we sowed the flower seeds. The asparagus is 3 inches above the ground. Eggplants will not thrive.

28th: Mrs. Gummidge commenced setting.

March 1st: Suffer exceedingly from indigestion all the time. No reading and little to do.

8th: A week ago I felt the child move within me for the first time, tho nearly five months of my time must have expired. Since this I enjoy myself much better—am no longer afflicted with nausea and heart burn. My life has been and is likely to be so free from excitement of every sort during this experience that the child if not stupid, should, at least, be equable in disposition. I am 34 years old and my husband either one or two years older. My mother was not married until her thirtieth year. I was her second child born three years afterwards. My sister, two years my senior, is thoroughly superficial and selfish—one of those persons who are mature as they will be at fifteen.

9th: Rained heavily last night—has been threatening some days. Potatoes and barley make quite a show.

14th: Spent yesterday afternoon with the Meaders—galloped there and felt invigorated by the exercise and change. Today Mr. and Mrs. Sawin came to see me and on returning were, I fear, caught in the rain which has come again heavily this afternoon. Last week Mrs. Meader sent me 4 or 5 pounds of her good butter, which is a great present here in these days, being a dollar a pound and not to be had at that.

15th: Rain is still coming down. I am not at all well, think a journal a stupid and heartless affair and have come to the conclusion that the peculiar characteristics of a child are the result of inmost indescribable and perhaps unrecognizable states of mind. While I write there is the heaviest hail storm I ever saw in my life—not excepting those of Canada, East.

25th: William Coleman came today in the coast steamer; he proposes looking at land in the Pajaro.[31]

27th: Sunday. C. went to the mission and the rain came on before he got there.

30th: Rain (heavy) ceased—river much swollen, wrote to Relief Buffum from whom I had heard lately.   Health somewhat improved. Many chickens to tend to.

April 7th: Sent letters to M. and W. Johnson and Eleanor Hill.[32] Spent part of Sunday and Monday at the Whitings'. Whiting is a shallow, conceited, dogmatic, insolent, pro-slavery braggart and I came home quite sad and hopeless about the progress of truth and justice in this country, where it is the universal custom to call sin virtue—to boast of oppression and brag of the freedom of this great country, all in a breath—to hate with a wolfish hatred those who dare to advocate the most obvious right, what reason have we for hope? I despair. I see nothing but approaching despotism in America and that not a century hence.
I should live where I can have the sympathy of abolitionists. It makes me bitter and cold and contemptuous, the mixing only with the shallow tyrant or timid apologist.   Mr. Bowman, also, has turned out quite other than he was represented and than he represented himself. He is coarse, gluttonous, and personally dirty, without self-respect, courage, or truthfulness. First he wearied me with flattery and blarney, then by his low meanness, so that I loathe his presence. He is mean, unmanly, and picayunish. K. is constantly expressing his annoyance at him and his regret at having engaged him, and this increases my feeling. I

am so keenly sensitive to the characters of those about me that I suffer and am too much engrossed with either the meannesses or virtues of my associates. It is unfortunate that these are my circumstances in these three last months. I can conceive of nothing worse. There is now a weekly mail from the Atlantic states.

16th: K. has gone to the Pajaro. I am pretty well, but for heart burn. Sent letters to Robert and Tacie. It seems strange that as my time of trial approaches I feel less anxiety about preparing for it than at first. Our garden begins to look ship-shape.

Sunday, April 17th: A severe rain storm last night, today a high wind.

29th: Violent rain storm last night. Heard by the mail of last week from Maggie Voorhees and Sarah Shaw.[33] Would that M. were with me.

May 1st: Sunday—Sprained my ankle pretty badly in stepping off the front piazza. Hobbled in, mixed some bread, and fed the youngest chickens so that matters might not stand quite so bad when K. and Tom return with the cow, which they did shortly. The Brown brothers spent the day with us. Health quite fair, especially since K. supplies me so well with candy of which I am extravagantly fond.

3rd: K. planted melons and many other things. Last night it showered a little. The opinion among intelligent persons is that the general cultivation of the soil is fast changing the climate.

15th: K. gone down to the Pajaro to make more certain of the nurse for me and to bring home the American cow he bought of Bryant. Our new Spanish cow, Adumblah, is quite good, giving 6 or 7 qts of most excellent milk per diem. Yesterday got letter from Moses and Mary Atwood, Alton, Ill., containing seeds, hop—malthea— Zinnia—Aster and others. Also one from Oliver Johnson, who leaves the *Freeman* for the *A. S. Standard*. [34] Tom killed a deer this morning. I, however, have disliked meat of every sort these many months—live on bread and milk and cream, to which lately may be added blackberries, of which I am extremely fond. Health pretty good—sadly wanting in mental concentration.

19th: Rain threatening again. Yesterday I did a very large washing that I had been putting off for months. The little fawn and the numerous broods of young chickens are a great trouble to me. I get so fatigued. Instead of the cow and certainty of a nurse, K. came home with a plan for selling out here and buying a large rancho in the Pajaro. I earnestly hope he may succeed in doing so, for I like the idea of a large landed estate and especially in the neighborhood of Bryant and Eleanor. I have made the best of acquaintances here but, alas, for friends. I shall feel more settled down there.

21st: Six visitors from the mission to dinner and tea. In the afternoon most of us turned out blackberrying. The berries we ate for supper with cream and sugar. I got my arms poisoned by ivy, pretty badly. They want me to return the compliment by passing Saturday and Sunday in town, but I feel that it would be imprudent to risk the fatigue of horseback riding and as yet we have no buggy.

29th: Mr. K. gone again to the Pajaro. I do not like the being left alone. Everything grows very fast, tho we have showers every week and coolish weather. On the 27th we sent out 40 bags of ripe potatoes and shall continue to dig more largely every week. A sort of caterpillar is making sad work of the potatoes, onions, etc., in most places, especially in the bottom lands near and in the mission. They cut them clean off to the root. As yet they have done us but little damage.

31st: Mr. Bowman at last gone to the tan yard to my eminent satisfaction. I only hope K. will get rid of him soon and I hope it will be a long time before I again accept a person on the character given them by another, belying my own strong impressions. The human voice is the truest index to the interior qualities of the soul. The manly, frank, clear-headed person has a voice pleasant to listen to; the timid one, time server, and scatter brains, quite another. Owing to Lucretia Mott's sweet and gracious social affections her voice is music itself, rich and never failing.[35] A person with merely her intellect, or with less affection, could by no possibility have such delicious intonations. Mr. Bowman's nasal, monotonous, blarneying voice so disgusted me that I never staid in his presence. I have not eaten at the table for three months, so much did his ill manners and gluttony annoy me.

The good nurse cannot leave home. I hate the idea of a doctor. Alas, if the child does not push his own way vigorously into the world it may go ill with me, but I hope and trust it [the child] will.

June 15th: All goes well. Two weeks ago we sent up our first ripe potatoes which brought 10 and 9˙ cts, last week more, and they brought 8 cts. Five hands are digging, ready for to-morrow's steamer. I am well enough to cook for so many with K's careful help in the way of preparation before he leaves for the yard. Indeed, just now, excepting for two or three hours in the forenoon, I feel badly; I can only doze away on the couch. I am well enough. The few debts will be paid, a piece of desirable land for a new tan yard in the "village" bought—a team, also, and a kitchen and barn put up. I can hardly hope for a buggy, and yet without one and with an infant I shall be sadly isolated.   I have read Thackeray's *Pendennis* and can see that there is great talent in the book, but it does not excite in me the least emotion, does not strengthen or enlighten me in any way.[36] I can see how it may be popular with those who have no interest in progress.

The flowers that are blossoming quite cheer me—the great sun flowers—African marigolds—poppies and princes feathers— the nasturtiums, too. Yellow, for some reason, always pleases me and in my rides a patch of yellow flowers in a green field invites my attention till I have quite passed it by.

Besides the chickens, turkies, dog (Nip), cat, and other live stock, K. has just had a present of a couple of English terriers— little, cunning things. The female will sit on her haunches and beg. He has such a hearty, boyish love of animals that altho I am sometimes inclined to rebel against the size of the family, I am reconciled again by a consideration of the beauty of such simple affections.

July 29th: Exactly two weeks after the preceding entry my little girl was born (June 29th, '53) between 11 and 12 a.m. (Ora Bruce Kirby).[37] It was at least ten days before the time I had calculated on. No nurse could by any possibility be obtained. K. had gone to the yard and I was expecting Mr. and Mrs. Meader to spend the day. They had been up the coast to try and engage some one and were now to report progress. I did not feel well on rising, and by the time the Meaders arrived I had to go to bed for good. It was fortunate that they came, for there was no woman nearer than the mission and when I should have sent off Tom to fetch Mr. K., I should have been entirely alone. For 24 hours I had a terrible time and had to take chloroform at last. Mrs. Meader remained till the babe was born and Mrs. Frick, the school-master's wife, was persuaded to come and stay with me for a week.[38] She is a conscientious, gentle, thoughtful person with many just, practical ideas, but weakly, inefficient, and untidy. In ten days she was bound to go home, and I, scarcely able to bear my own weight, must take the entire charge of the infant and, to some extent, of the house. K. and Tom do all they possibly can, but the former must see to the yard and Tom is busy with the other hands digging potatoes. Now the baby is a month old, she cries much at night and that keeps me from getting strong. My breasts, too, are gathering, so that my life is pretty much a misery, physically speaking, and all because those stupid doctors had no breast pump to drain my milk.

There is considerable excitement just now about the discovery of gold at Siant and the Rincon and other places in the neighborhood.[39] It has never been found in sufficient quantities as yet to pay for the digging, but now they say they can get $5 a day and that is fair wages. However we do not feel at all certain as to the truth of the case.

July [Aug?] 19th: Baby has had a slight eruption on her since she was three days old. I hope that it will leave of its own accord. I fancy, also, that she has a cast in the left eye, which, if so, was caused by bringing her suddenly into too strong light. She has ruptured herself by crying hard when I was too ill to be able to use the ordinary means of pacifying her. Otherwise she is strong and well—very wakeful, tho. How entirely I am divested of leisure hours or even moments now. When Ora is not in my arms I see so many things that I ought to do and that I should like to do that it destroys the satisfaction of doing anything. I am beginning to feel like myself again. I lanced my right breast myself and in a week I hope it will be healed.

Sept. 10th: It is sometime now since I heard from Byberry, and I feel deserted and lonely. Besides, our pecuniary affairs are in no flourishing condition. The rapid decline in the price of potatoes made the two last shipments a loss and now the worms (a species of maggot) have got at all the late crop, both in the near and off hollows and these potatoes will not sell at all, and, indeed, will soon be eaten hollow. The potato crop throughout the valleys and on the coast is a total failure through this worm. It throws us back so—no ready money and various bills for labor due. These considerations, with Mrs. F's dishonorable conduct making Mr. K. liable for $2,000 next spring and summer, keep me in a state of unrest. If we were only quite out of debt with no danger threatening distinctly in the distance I should be as happy as possible.

Nov. 5th: The winter rains are delayed. Mr. K. goes to San F. tomorrow to sell leather. Tom Purdy, the nice English lad, has come to live with us. Baby is well as it is possible for a child to be and has been so for the last two months. She is remarkably strong, especially on the back and is so very happy in her existence that I quite envy her, wishing I myself were a child again and so cared for. She scarcely ever cries and usually smiles gleefully when ever I look at her. She observes much for her age, loves to be out of doors early in the morning when the deer and other animals are about. I am wholly satisfied in the child who has health, strength, intellect, and good nature. Dr. McLean has done me good service in curing the rupture.[40] She is, indeed, the light of the household. Her father takes great pride and pleasure in her. I have forgotten my great suffering and wish for two more children—one girl and one boy—the latter to please my husband only, for I love girls best. Mr. K. has some idea of giving up farming and devoting himself to the raising of pigs, chickens, and vegetables and it would gratify me to have him do so, for I fear his health will fail totally by the severe labor of the yard. If he were to live wholly on the farm he would be constantly improving it in some way—would plant an orchard— make a duck-pond and vineyard, build a large barn, and finish and improve the house. We should have a fine flower garden and all sorts of conveniences.

Lately I have been reading "The Caxtons" over again. I am more than struck by the true wisdom embodied in it. Thackeray's books are all aimless, superficial, and unimproving to me. *Vanity Fair* has poor contrast in the mutely amiable Amelia and Captain Dobbin.[41] Mrs. Stowe's, "Key" Sumner's books, and the anti-slavery literature generally is of quite another stamp. Without this connecting link I could not live so far from any centre of thought. My mind would shrink to the modicum of those with whom I associate and growth be a mere word in the dictionary. The *Tribune* and *A. S. Standard* do indeed supply me with the bread of life.

Nov. 28th: Mr. K. has been absent now more than three weeks and I have for the last ten days endured the most horrible anxiety. I cannot care for the housekeeping or anything else. The first heavy rains came on the 24th (Thursday) and today only has it ceased. I force myself to eat for the baby's sake. Our new "Tom" loves the baby and is also very cheerful, but until this load is off my mind I cannot appreciate mirthfulness.

The heavy rains and my distance from the mission, with only a lad of seventeen in the house and he without a saddle, prevent me from taking such measures and making such inquiries as would afford me temporary relief—oh, that he may be home by tomorrow night having suffered only temporary sickness. Letters from Robert Purvis and Tacie Townsend (24th), showing that John Bowman's real character has come to light. Letter from Maggie by the preceding mail—she will not come.

Jan. 25th, '54: Little one thrives—is remarkably strong and healthy. In December after K.'s return I took her to the mission and made a visit of a few days to Mrs. Farnham who was down on account of Eddy's sickness and of Mr. Hobson, who has since died. She has a beautiful baby girl [with] a splendid head and a joyous generous face. The babe is 4 days younger than mine. By comparing I find Ora's head lacking in breadth—imagination and cautiousness—she is wide between the eyes which Mrs. F. says Redfield says is music.[42] Ora never takes cold tho much exposed early and late out of doors at her father's coming and going. She is so nervously active and yet so strong that I hope much from her mental activities, so sustained. I love Mrs. F. inspite of the anxiety and trouble she has caused us and may yet, by her past culpable action. How I long for a more intellectual life. Now that my motherly nature is gratified I long to turn to study. Ora is well; that if it were not for household drudging I could study with her very easily.

May 25, 1855: Sixteen months have elapsed since the last entry. Rather a wearisome, hopeless time—pecuniary difficulties make such hard work for the honest minded. Last December we moved to the mission leaving Tom as tenant on the farm which we had been unable to sell. Since January the new tan yard has been in successful operation and we are living in a droll little white-washed house not five minutes walk from it.[43] Ora is nearly two years old— hearty as ever. Three months ago I miscarried from over-exertion— but find myself enceinte again and so am desirous of recording my circumstances and states of minds in order the better to learn the effect of these on the character of the child.

I have no leisure for the quiet dreaming that occupied me so much before Ora's birth and yet my mind is no more clear or orderly. For a long time the music seems to have died out of me—no melody, no sense of rhythm. I am tired and stupid of doing all my own work for so long. Mr. K. is also quite exhausted with the close application of four years. He looks older by ten years and is easily attacked by sickness now. Mrs. Farnham has taught our common school for the last five months and if she continues we may hope something for the place.

Aug. '55: My health is pretty good with the exception of the inevitable results of prolapsis. I must be full five months toward my time. For the last two, my mind has been tolerably active, after the dry Yankee sort—better only than stagnation. The child, if I continue thus, must have more force, more ordinary intellect than Ora and less delicacy, less originality, less music, less physical health or activity. All hope of growth in Santa Cruz through Mrs. Farnham's influence in the public school is at an end. Little Mary, who was four days younger than Ora and possessed of a wonderful brain, died of acute water on the brain last month and her mother bereft of her only consolation was unequal to the task of drudging through the few remaining months of her school year—the rowdies again have matters in their own hands and a low-bred ignoramus teaches a private school.   In October, doubtless, the narrow-minded, sanctimonious Frick will again vent his spite on the children of the district. I have taken, through Mr. Cutler of San F., the first steps towards procuring liberal Unitarian teaching for those of us who cannot accept the sorry Methodism.[44] I long to be teaching somebody myself, but there is not sufficient appreciation of the higher sort of culture to make any parent anxious to part with even one out of six girls. The question still, could I be of service to my kind elsewhere? I am of none here.

Have the whooping cough—took it from Ora. Never had a cough before—feel weak in the day from coughing so much at night—have cramp in both chest and abdomen when coughing violently.

I preserve a tolerably cheerful, hopeful, and equable state of mind and am less over-tasked lately, having no man to board and no chickens to wait on. Ora, too, grows less troublesome, but I have let her have her own way too much.

During the four most important months of this pregnancy I had a class of girls for three hours each day. Those that really interested me were Maria and Ellen Hecox and Katherine Imus.[45] They went through "Combe's Constitution of Man," and we used to have all sorts of discussions with it.[46] The Methodist minister tells the parents that none but infidels believe in phrenology and that this is an infidel book. It is quite common here for girls to be engaged at twelve and marry at fourteen, so I and Mrs. Farnham (who came to me after Mary's death) endeavor to impress upon them the great truths bearing on marriage, maternity—the moral and physical laws affecting children and so forth. They accept the truths as self evident, but are met at home with the dogma that God for special purposes of his own takes babies away from their mothers and that it has nothing to do with what they eat or didn't wear.

I met with great opposition from Mr. Kirby about these girls coming to me, but I like to teach and knew that it would be beneficial to the child, keeping my mind clear and practical and active instead of dreary. Mrs. Farnham's presence, too, is the greatest blessing. We are so suggestive to each other. Every thing is as I could wish, excepting that fat is troublesome and having miscarried so lately I cannot take much exercise.

My own greatest want is self-esteem and concentrativeness. When I do what I am sure is right, I suffer for fear of the opinion of others, and if my friends don't write to me I fear they have become tired or disgusted with me. Then, too, I fly constantly from one subject to another, cannot think consecutively. To alleviate the effects of this I oblige myself to study geometry for one hour or so every evening. Finally I get quite engrossed with it. This I have done for months. So with this and Mrs. F. and the class I hope to give more intellect and more character to the child. I trembled every time K. saw the girls. He threatened to order them out of the house—said their parents would abuse me as they had Mrs. F. and tell lies about me—that people would say he could not support me and so forth. It was only by the greatest calmness and firmness that I avoided trouble and all for the sake of the result.

July 18, 1858: The above refers to Georgie's pre-natal circumstances. She was born on the 12th of December, 1855 and was the quietest and best of babies, apparently perfectly well, only the left eye was weak which I attribute to my having done so much sewing, especially as my eyes are quite weak when enceinte.

Cornelia was born in December '57 (at Sta Cruz Mission). I was in more comfortable circumstances before her birth, but had no intimate friends near me and no one to teach. In the first place there were no young persons who were of the sort that interested me belonging to persons who would trust a heretic with them, and then I found myself pretty fully occupied with caring for my two children and household generally. I occupied myself with sewing, constructing, planning garments of one sort or another, was very quiet and contented having nothing to vex me, also nothing to exercise my mental faculties as I had with Georgie. Cornelia is even a better, pleasant tempered child than Georgie, but I fear she will be more delicate in her organization, have less power of resistance and endurance. I read only one book that called out any thought, Guizot's "Civilization of Modern Europe."[47] A certain portion of geometry having served my purpose before I quite lost my interest in it and could not get it up again. If I could have laid hold of other histories equally fine with the above it would have answered my purpose, close attention being needed to comprehend and remember the events. I had a chimney and fireplace built in the home room, which at once reconciled me to the house I had before so disliked. I hope I shall not have another child, for I am sensible that my constitution is not what it was. From the time Ora was born I did not work until Georgie was six months old, not being at all equal to it, it seemed to drag me down so as I can never recover from it. I keep pretty well as long as I keep quiet, but directly I exert myself I get ill. During the three years I allude to it was a constant strain on my powers, bodily and mental. I used to wash at the tub when I trembled all over from weakness constantly, and it was so discouraging to go to bed at night feeling that notwithstanding such exertions the work was all behindhand. Ora was a most troublesome child till she was 3 1/2 or 4 years old. No one could imagine the mischief such a really good child could accomplish. Then to cook, wash, iron, houseclean, bake, mend, nurse, write letters, receive and pay visits, read, etc., all of which was necessary if I would really live like a civilized being, was too much for one person. I feel that at forty my constitution is gone and even if I had a boy he would not be what we should expect.

The children, Georgie and Ora, spend most of the time gathering bouquets in the garden and arranging them in cups, bottles and whatnot, and so every day.

It is more than three years since I spoke to Mr. Cutler of San F. about a Unitarian minister. He promised to write east and see what could be done. K. promised to board a person and give $100 a year besides, and we could easily have raised $1,000 more. Perhaps Mr. C. did his best but I never heard anything from him. Now the Congregationalists and Presbyterians have united and have quite a thriving church, but I do not believe the cause of true religion is helped by the ministrations of Mr. Zelie, who is a rigid sort of person without any flow of life or intellect or heart.[48] All his sermons are delivered in a loud, unmaterial tone of voice and none of them are on Christian virtues but all on the dogmas of the church. Last Sunday he proved to his own satisfaction that morality, love, charity, benevolence, etc., were not of the slightest use to save a man from Hell, only belief that you deserved to be damned and then accepted Christ as a saviour somehow. It must be very much easier and so require less ability to dish up doctrines in this way than to enlarge for an hour on brotherly love, peace-making, patience, teachableness, humility, or such subjects, making them pointed and interesting. For my part, believing that this is to be my home I shall not cease to work in every possible way to procure liberal teaching for those that will accept it. Mr. Gannett has sent me a number of tracts on the questions at issue between the liberal and orthodox Christians.[49] I have previously circulated all of Parker's sermons that I could command, and especially all sorts of general literature tending to a reasonable and affectionate and intelligent state of mind, such as W. Ware's works, the nobler poets, Judd's "Margaret," the best modern novels, and especially the noble anti-slavery literature of the day.[50] Now I am going at the *doctrines;* controversy is forever necessary at first to clear people's minds from false theories. The state of people who believe that religion consists in belief in certain dogmas must be vastly different from those who believe that religion is charity (St. Paul's) in the soul.

I am so perplexed about my children. I long to teach and so improve other children and I could, even now, do a little, say take two who needed help most or who would be more surely benefitted, for I have a most excellent girl, Anna McGee, who takes every bit of the household care as well as labor off my hands. I have the baby and children to see to, it is true, but I could do something and Ora would learn more willingly and be happier if she saw others, but I am deterred by the fear of exposing her to the influence of such manners and such coarse states of mind as I find in the lower class of children and none of the better class happen to have any. I shall certainly write to Mr. Gannett to see if he can help me to a religious teacher. The trouble is we sympathize with Theodore Parker and so do the most influential Unitarians of the place, and I fear the association would send us a conservative (so called) person.

July 25th, 1858: This week Mr. Zelie's adherents held a "festival," as they call it, in order to get money for the church furniture, the church, itself, being finished. There was a supper, a post-office, and a "grab-bag" for entertainment and it all went off extremely well. They cleared above expenses $330. All the town was there with the exception of Miss Mead and her sister, Mrs. Kittridge, whose husband, the Dr. is at variance with Mr. Farrand and the latter took a leading part in the festival.[51] After taking Miss M. home Judge Blackburn returned. Ora was so sleepy, and we eat the good things with our fingers. I heard last week that there was a fuss in the common school at Watsonville about two colored children, nice, intelligent, well-behaved children all say, but disgraced by their skin. I understand that the children are admitted but put off by themselves, poor things, and not allowed to take places no matter how much they out-spelled those above them. The more violently pro-slavery do not permit their children to go to the school at all. The ignorant, white people from the slave states are the curse of California, they are so stupid and so conceited they think one man (to-wit, themselves) just as good as another, providing there be not the least drop of African blood in them. I sent down "Ida May" and "Caste" to help the right side.[52]

This spring Mrs. Voorhees came with her two boys, Hermann and Theodore, and spent two months with us.[53] Her conversation is very charming to me and as we both lived many years at Margate in Kent, and have been about the same number of years in the United States, it is pleasant to compare notes. She is an artist. I am simply one who loves to help develop character and intellect aright. I am deficient in imagination, taste, delicacy. We have had separate existences, so different, yet we find much in common. She adds more to my life than I can to hers for I accept her views of the meaning and value of music—the cause and influence of a true architecture and so forth and she does not see as I do that anti-slavery is the great question of the day and the necessity of giving our hearty cooperation towards its downfall. I fear Theodore will not become the man she expects him to. Hermann will exceed her hopes. The last two years have given me many pleasant friends whom I hope to keep. Miss Ellis, who is now engaged to Mr. Jones, Mrs. Voorhees, and Mr. Jones, whom I feel more intimate with than formerly.[54] No one, tho, begins to fill Mrs. Farnham's place. Mrs. V. and I are anxious in the same way about our children. We see the evils of a new country with no old institutions, no grand old buildings, and seldom the best intellects and characters to call out reverence.

Nov. 15th, 1858: I have arrived at the most nervous and anxious

condition of mind and both on Georgie's account. It seems to me that
I have not slept a good sound whole night's sleep since Ora was
born. Georgie has a rather delicate and highly sensitive organism,
vim not withstanding. She looks so well. She has settled weakness
of the bowels—has always had, and I only wonder she keeps up at
all. I sleep with her in order to keep her covered, fearing that a
chill would react on the bowels. I attend scrupulously to her diet,
exercise, clothing. She wore flannel drawers and jacket and high
necked dresses and thick shoes. Inspite of all this care she gets
weaker and her condition does not impove at all. I have no heart
for anything and the loss of rest (for she is very restless at night)
takes all the strength out of me. There is not one person of
cultivated, enlarged mind in the place. Sometimes I seem quite
collapsed for the want of spiritual food. Zelie I cannot go to hear.
He is by nature a hard, vindictive, tyrannical, mechanical sort of
person without the principle of growth in him at all. He talks
about grace and change of heart, but I don't know any one who needs
those things more than he does, or one whom the change is less
possible to. Never a sermon on patience, quietness, love, tenderness
or pity, but law, the terrors of the law, the fear of God, etc.

Jan. 5th, 1859: This year opens with one blessing at least for me. I
have found a cure for Georgie's weakness in castile soap and brandy.
But also I hear that Mrs. F will not return to Cal, although I have
all along believed that her proper place was among more advanced
minds and characters than those here. I am at once led to ask
"What then am I to do? How can I live?" The moving spirit of Cal.
is an external one; the prominent traits—generosity, cheerfulness,
hope—but no love of abstract ideas, no tendency to seek for truth.
The thriving are happily engrossed with their happy
circumstances; those who do not thrive are too sadly conscious of
their poor estate to care for the higher life of the soul.

Speaking from the ordinary standpoint, I say Santa Cruz is
a most excellent place, containing worthy, intelligent people and
yet I feel myself utterly alone. Indeed since my marriage I never
felt so lonely as this fall and winter.

Dr. Burrell and family from Sacto.[Sacramento] will have
settled here within a few weeks. I find him an excellent physician
and most reliable and gentlemanly man. His wife is not equal to

him but quite tolerable. Something she told me about her state of mind previous to the birth of her first child convinces me that the most deplorable consequences result when the pregnant woman entertains antipathy even if that antipathy is perfectly justifiable in itself, being the dislike and disgust for what is in its very nature detestable. It is a constant shutting up of ones sympathies instead of pouring them out on all sides, thus giving your child large and generous sympathies. Oh, if men as well as women did but know how much depends on this fact, how the husband would endeavor to call into play all his wife's nobler qualities, stimulating and aiding her in controlling her weaknesses and improving her powers in every way.

Jan. 30th, '59: Within the last seven or eight weeks our young neighbor James Morgan became raving mad and finally died at the asylum at Stockton.[55] He was a remarkably reasonable and conscientious young man and became insane from his inability to experience the sudden change from despair to joy that Methodists call "getting religion." He was too well balanced to be carried away by emotion and yet being wholly within the orthodox and mostly the Methodist atmosphere he was impressed that he was in a wrong and dangerous state until he did so. He had remarkable concentrativeness. Finally when Mr. (Elder) Briggs brought his magnetism to bear on him and made a powerful appeal to the audience to escape the wrath to come, he went immediately mad.[56] Such cases would more frequently occur were the irrational dogmas of the church, total depravity and eternal punishment, more truly believed, but fortunately they live only in the brain and the heart is unblighted by them.

 This event will still further increase the unpopularity of the Methodist form of religion, for altho the Presbyterian, which is and is likely to be dominant for some years at least, entertains exactly the same dogmas, it appeals less to the passions.

 I do not see, on looking back, that I have mentioned anything of Maria or Ellen Hecox, two daughters of Mrs. Adna Hecox, who, of the young girls before alluded to, especially interested me. Maria I had much to do with—taught her for a time French and German especially, generally instructed her in morals, manners, and so forth. She was neat, bright, affectionate, brave, impulsive. As she outgrew the narrow Methodist set, her mother became disturbed and ended by hating and insulting me. Ellen had more intellect but less character than her elder sister. She was well read for her years and possessed great talent, I might say genius, for drawing heads, animals, etc. In order to withdraw her from me the mother urged her into a marriage with a low fellow, one Cap. Watson, when she was scarcely fourteen. Maria took her destiny into her own hands, went to San F. to school, then to Sacramento into Cornelius Cole's family and finally married a Dr. Tilden when she was nearly seventeen. I missed the pleasant labor of instructing Maria.[57] Now, Jan '59, I have taken Mary Jane Morgan, another undisciplined child of fourteen.[58] She is infinitely less developed for her age than either of the others, indeed, has naturally less intellect. She cannot even read intelligently, and of books of any sort is quite ignorant, but she is capable, active, very pretty and tho irreverent like all the western children, is teachable and seems to be glad to do a little for herself. The western children are so generally fine looking, they have more constitution than the Yankees—have what the English call in their horses "bottom"—that I should like to have the training of them all, even as they are. Miss Mary Jane says to me at the breakfast table "There is a hair in the apple sauce, I believe it is one of yours by the color." She talks a lot of rambling nonsense, calls my friends by their Christian names, and pronounces her wretched English in such a shocking manner that sometimes I give up and think I will try not to be interested in her, but that is nonsense, for I cannot help myself.

April 14, '59: Miss Mary Jane proved a failure. Neither she, nor indeed any of the family but the one who died lately and the oldest, Joseph, have any worthy ambition. I have tried the youngest, Salome, who is now ten years old and cannot read the first of the Rollo books.[59] She staid away on the least excuse and no one at home paid any attention to her coming over at the right hour. Tot and she are great friends and I wished to arouse in her some desire of improvement but failed. Ora is too intelligent to be satisfied with ignorance in a friend. They represent pretty well the "poor white trash" of the slave states where the parents were born and married. Get up late, dawdle about and do forever a long string of nothings. Let all the children drink tea and coffee and up as late as the parents. Live principally on buckwheat cakes, send the children to school a week and keep them out two months, borrow incessantly everything from indigo to a pair of stockings to go to a party in. I believe I've given up trying to do anything for them.

I do my own work with K's help and a woman to wash. Am growing by degrees much more cheerful and at rest, not so frantic as I used to be for want of the finest people for friends. Begin to realize that a little progress is a good thing and it's no use looking for strides. Besides the children grow to be less babies and demand the sort of attention that needs more mind. K. is more respectful than he used to be. Has left off sneering at me and is really becoming considerate and tender. The children are in fine health. I delight to see the garden so well planted, anticipate a forest about me. Ora reads in Epes Sargent's 2nd reader—to herself, also, the history of General Tom Thumb, the idea of whom seems to interest her extremely. These with Peter Spekter's Fables and the history of Five Little Pigs comprise all her library.[60] Georgie is between three and four and talks such a lingo none of us can always interpret.

Sept. 24th, '59: Mrs. Farnham has returned to Cal. and to us. I was in San F. early in July and felt myself alive once more on meeting her. She has greatly improved in the three years (tho I was quite satisfied with her before), being more patient of the low condition of what is called civilization, with a quieter spirit, greater intellectual ability, and unabated zeal in the cause of larger truths. Her manner of advocating spiritualism is very effective. She has lectured (principally on these religious views) every Sunday evening nearly since she came down. Also she had a class of women, the most respectable in the place, to whom she gave "conversations" on her view of woman. It being that woman is superior, spiritually, to man. This she proves by the added organs and functions, the greater delicacy of organization, greater beauty and the fact that she holds a large—immense—balance of power over the character of her off-spring. Mrs. Kittridge, Blackburn, Egleston, Porter and Taylor—Roberts, Smith, Rawson and myself attended and yet Dr. Rawson, for some unknown reason, has given himself up to circulating the vilest reports of her teachings.[61]

These disgustingly sensual views are listened to and believed by large numbers, notwithstanding that the members of the class are indignant to the last degree, as her teachings enlighten and strengthen those who attend (Sundays). The church is not aided thereby and sectarian virulence abounds against her. There are very few actual church members, but these have the will to roast her at the stake. Deacon Wm. Anthony says she is a "She Devil"; Mrs. Ruffner that "she is worse than the keeper of a brothel."[62] Dr. Rawson circulates the most scandalous lies purporting to come from her. These are all leaders in the Congregational Church. But she has steadily good audiences and makes as earnest friends as enemies by her most valuable services. She extemporises always, commands her hearers unbroken attention from the first moment to the last. Her large philosophical brain, her tender, religious, womanly nature carry conviction to all capable of progress.

Just as she entered upon these Sunday lectures, a young man admirably fitted for the task commenced the publication of the "Santa Cruz News."[63] There had been a local paper published here these two years, but it was beneath criticism. The selections consisting nearly always of the most gross and disgusting anecdotes and the editorials minus. Slocum of the News published in his first number a good report of Mrs. F.'s second lecture. Then such a storm as poured on his head. The pious complained, threatened, abused, as usual. The very few courageous encouraged. Slocum is a refined, intuitive, manly fellow, but lacking the ability to battle with the external world. It is impossible for him to lower his standard, to back down from his position. He suffers terribly from want of sympathy, want of means, inability to cope with and over-power this violent, coarse tirade made upon him. We cheer him all we can. God send that he may be sustained, that freedom and truth may thereby be helped. He has gone down to the Pajaro to get subscribers.

Mrs. F. and Mr. Kirby both went to the City on the 25th inst[ant] Mrs. S. M. Clarke, an intellectual, useful woman will die of prostration caused by Uterine disease if nothing can be done in the use of electricity for her.[64] She believes Mrs. F. can do this and so the latter reluctantly leaves for a while her writer's work (a book on woman, her uses, position, destiny, and so forth) with the incidental work of her lecturing every Sunday, to go and see if she can be helped.

Dr. Burrell, having not a particle of earnestness or courage and being fond of persons lower in tone than himself, preferred acceding to the false and base reports as to her character, experience, etc. The Joneses considered it impolite and inadvisable to countenance a public woman. They became very thick with the B's, but finally Mrs. Jones was too good to stand the hollowness of their lives, the animal stupid children resulting therefrom, and the gross neglect of said children's highest good, and has virtually rebelled. Still I can see she has the slavish feeling that a good wife must not outgrow her husband—must not take any stand, however gently and kindly.

Eleanor Hill spent some months with us this fall. I was dreadfully wearied by her dead level of dullness, her absolute dislike of any thing or person beyond mediocrity—an endless flow of talk on cooking, housekeeping generally, dresses, sickness. I saw how bad her influence had been on Ella—never by any possibility appealing to nobility, elevation of character. She will be neat, orderly, externally polite, intelligent, hard, selfish, material. If we could organize a circle and have some physical demonstrations even, it would help our side among such an undeveloped set, wonderfully.

Ora has improved in disposition wonderfully within the last three months. She has laid aside her defiant tone, is more reverent and affectionate. In fact a most willing and capable child. I hope the great trial is at last over. I never doubted her radical goodness, but the wilfulness and apparent unimpressiblity destroyed my peace to a very serious extent.

28th, '59: Today Deacon Wm. Anthony wrote to Mr. Slocum to stop his paper, "he did not wish it to be read by his family." They are real puritans and have the spirit that a century or so ago would have roasted people. S. meets with so little encouragement here that he thinks of moving to the Pajaro where as yet there is no paper. They offer to raise $500 by subscription if he will go there. Materially it is a far better place to this and will be of more importance by reason of its larger population. Among this greater number of persons greater aid to the paper is possible.

The women in Watsonville are an uncultivated,

undeveloped set. It is bad enough here but it is fifty times worse there. However, I consider it a gain that no orthodox church is yet permanently established there.   There are (nominally) two Methodist churches, the M. E. C. North and the M. E. C. South. The latter permitted Mrs. F. to lecture in their house (not on religion). She described the small room as being lined with smooth blacked cloth. There were no tin reflectors or other arrangements for candles. These they melted a little, dropping the grease on the desk or bench back and quickly clapping the candle down on it to stick. This fact indicates the sort of civilization that [is] there.

Yesterday's "Times" contains the account of the meeting for erecting a monument to Broderick.[65] The Republican want of courage and clear sightedness was seen in their shutting down discussion of the man's life, opinions, etc., and deciding to put on the monument "The son of a stone-cutter, a Senator from California," as if his great influence and superiority consisted in these facts at all. Plenty of mechanics arrive at places in this country and yet are unworthy of the admiration of any decent man—many deserve and obtain the contempt of the wise and good. If they had put his name, simply, it would have been better than this flummery. He was an advanced man—not a man of the future, but he helped others in his own position in independence.

Jan. 26th, 1860: "The News" still continues its starved existence. People are so slow to exert themselves—even those whose sympathies are right. A few say it, the paper, must not stop, as it could never be resuscitated when needed for the next Presidential election. I found myself enceinte in September, '59 and went to the city to refresh my soul for the effort. The mountain road was in shocking condition which coming on my already irritated and weak state caused a severe miscarriage in the city, from which I but slowly recovered. In my invalid condition I saw much of dear Margaret Voorhees who was indefatigable in her care and devotion. I saw a good deal of George Brooks and enjoyed his lively interest in spiritualism. He is to visit us soon.

The Voorhees have gone to New York as Mrs. Sinclair finally comes into possession of her alimony.[66] I fear they may make arrangements that will preclude their return.

My thoughts in those days ran on the freedom of women—on

what slaves we are and have been to the decisions of men. A hundred years hence it will be looked on with astonishment that a woman is prevented by public opinion from having a child unless she finds someone whom she wishes to accept as master for life.

Notes

The Journal of Georgiana Bruce Kirby

1. The popular, nineteenth-century theory that a pregnant mother's thoughts influenced her unborn child's mental, emotional, and physical development had been presented to Georgiana Bruce Kirby (hereafter GBK) through the writings of the Scottish phrenologist George Combe (1788–1858) and through the lectures of the English educator Charles Lane (1800–1870). GBK met Lane in 1843, when he visited Brook Farm. That same year Lane founded with Bronson Alcott, father of author Louisa May Alcott, the utopian colony Fruitlands, near Harvard, Massachusetts. Georgiana Bruce Kirby, *Years of Experience: An Autobiographical Narrative* (New York: Putnam, 1887), p. 153. The "Tom" to whom GBK refers may be Thomas Boyds, who in the 1852 California State Census is listed following the Kirbys as being a 28-year-old farmer, born in Missouri.

2. Richard Cornelius Kirby was born in 1817, a year before GBK, in Staffordshire, England. He served a seven-year apprenticeship in the leather trade before leaving for the United States in 1842. After working first in New York and then in New London, Connecticut, he signed aboard a whaling ship bound for the coast of Asia. He later jumped ship, finding his way to Astoria, Oregon, in 1845. He tanned leather for a time at Oregon City, before leaving for California. After much illness and adversity he arrived in San Francisco. He dressed leather for Captain John A. Sutter at Sutter's Fort, near Sacramento, and then returned to San Francisco, where he bought a lot near North Beach and established a small tan yard. In the winter of 1847–1848, he accepted the offer of William Blackburn to work in his tan yard on Joseph Majors's Rancho San Agustin (Scotts Valley). He went to the mines in the gold rush, but returned to Santa Cruz after losing

money in unwise investments. In the fall of 1850, he established a small tan yard at Squabble Hollow (Glen Canyon). On March 23, 1852, he married GBK. *Santa Cruz County, California: Illustrations Descriptive of Its Scenery, Fine Residences, Public Buildings, Manufactories, Hotels. . . .* (San Francisco: Wallace W. Elliott & Co., 1879) (hereafter SCC), pp. 24–26; John Henry Brown, *Early Days of San Francisco, California* (Oakland: Biobooks, 1949), p. 134.

3. The Kirbys obtained their first ranch through the popular "squatter's rights," used by many Yankees who created homesteads on unoccupied lands. The practice was an infringement upon the title holdings of the native Californios, who were forced to prove ownership of their ranchos through battle in the courts. Though the exact location of the ranch which GBK named "La Salud" (good health) is unknown, it was situated in the area of Blackburn Gulch (today's Branciforte Drive area), two miles from the tan yard and three miles northeast of the Mission Santa Cruz. Kirby traveled regularly to the mission plaza to arrange for the purchase and shipment of hides. References to the "mission" are to the little village of Santa Cruz, which had grown up around the Mission Santa Cruz, founded in 1791. In 1850, Santa Cruz County had a population of 643; by 1860 the population had grown to 4,944.

4. Reuben H. Sawin came to Santa Cruz in 1849, from New Orleans, where he was in the furniture business with William Blackburn. It was Blackburn, through his friend Henry Speale, who invited Sawin to come to Santa Cruz to help him finish a sawmill he was building in Blackburn Gulch. By 1850 the mill was operating, but there was already a glut of lumber to San Francisco. Sawin planted a crop of potatoes near present downtown Santa Cruz and moved in 1850 to a farm two miles "up the coast" from the town. In 1868 he built a home on Mission Street. Both Reuben and his wife, Sarah S., are buried in Evergreen Cemetery. SCC, p. 27.

5. Pasear (Spanish), literally, to walk for amusement; in this sense it is used as an expression for a pleasure trip.

6. Hiram Imus, a Connecticut veteran of the War of 1812, was the patriarch of a large family who settled in Santa Cruz County before 1850. Leon Rowland, *Santa Cruz, The Early Years: The Collected Historical Writings of Leon Rowland* (Santa Cruz: Paper Vision Press, 1980) (hereafter SCE), p. 144. The Hecox family, Adna A. and Margaret with their four children, Sarah, Catherine Maria, Margaret Ellen, and Adna H., left Illinois for California in 1846. Their first child, Evelyn, had died in

Illinois. Five other children were later born to the Hecoxes, Matilda, James, Alwilda, Laura, and Orville. Margaret M. Hecox, *California Caravan: The 1846 Overland Trail Memoir.* . . . edited and with introduction by Richard Dillon (San Jose: Harlan-Young Press, 1966), pp. 63-64. Hecox was a storekeeper with Elihu Anthony. He also was a lay minister of the Methodist Episcopal Church and helped establish the first Methodist Church in Santa Cruz, as well as several temperance societies. He was elected alcalde (mayor) of the Santa Cruz District in 1849 and later held many other local government offices. He became keeper of the Santa Cruz lighthouse in 1869, the position he held until his death in 1883, when his daughter Laura assumed the post. Frank Perry, *Lighthouse Point; Reflections on Monterey Bay History* (Soquel, CA: GBH Publishing, 1982), pp. 41–46, 59. Silas Bennett had met Elihu Anthony at Coloma in gold country and came with him to Santa Cruz in 1850. The Bennetts lived on Mission Street opposite Union Street. SCE, pp. 146–147. The Hollenbeck family lived on the grounds of what is today Santa Cruz High School. John Chase, *The Sidewalk Companion to Santa Cruz Architecture*, rev. ed. (Santa Cruz: Paper Vision Press, 1979) (hereafter SWC), p.256. Elihu and Sarah A. Anthony came to California in 1847 from Indiana and to Santa Cruz in 1848. He engaged in trade and real estate and built the first wharf in 1849. He also established the first foundry which made the first cast iron plow ever constructed in California. At this foundry were also made the first mining picks that were used in the gold fields. He was active in the Methodist Episcopal Church and was a member of the first County Board of Supervisors, elected in 1852. SCC, p. 29. Moses A. Meader (also spelled Meder and Meeder) came to California in 1846 by ship with the Sam Brannan party of Mormons. He first worked for Isaac Graham, repairing his sawmill on Zayante Creek. He later rented Graham's San Lorenzo sawmill and became prosperous through profitable lumber sales. He acquired the Rancho Refugio from José Bolcoff, a Russian who had come to California in 1815. Meader's wife, Sarah D. Blood, died in 1872. His daughter was named Angeline. SCC, p. 30. Mary Amney Case and her husband, Benjamin Allen Case, crossed the plains with Elihu Anthony in 1847. She started the first school in Santa Cruz in 1848 in her home on the edge of today's Nearys Lagoon. The Cases lost their savings in a hotel venture in Los Angeles in 1869. Mary Case eventually returned to Santa Cruz, where she died in 1900. SCE, pp.138, 148.

7. José Antonio Rodriguez and Joaquin Castro were the founders of the two families who through land grants eventually owned a quarter of a million acres in what is now Santa Cruz County. Maria de los Angeles Castro, Joaquin's daughter, married Joseph Majors. SCE, pp. 37–38.

8. James W. Brier, the first full-time minister of the Methodist Episcopal Church in Santa Cruz, had crossed the plains from Michigan by way of Death Valley in 1849. The story of James and his wife Juliette's harrowing journey with their three young sons can be found in Robert Glass Cleland, *From Wilderness to Empire* (New York: Alfred Knopf, 1962), pp. 132–133.

9. H. S. Loveland was the first teacher at the Methodist Academy, "who seems to have failed utterly in maintaining a character to warrant such a position." C. V. Anthony, *Fifty Years of Methodism: A History of the Methodist Episcopal Church* (San Francisco: Methodist Book Concern, 1901) (hereafter FYM), p. 79.

10. Thomas Russell, a forty-niner, had come to Santa Cruz soon after Eliza and took over farming her land when she failed at it. He was mysteriously murdered in a gulch near Evergreen Cemetery in 1856. Kirby eventually bought the Farnham land from Eliza's son Charles and sold part of it to Russell's son, Alexander. SCE, p. 141.

11. James Bryant Hill arrived in California in the Pajaro Valley in 1851. Rowland states that he had been in charge of farming at Brook Farm ten years before. In November, 1851, he leased 2,000 acres of choice farming land in the Pajaro Valley from Manuel Jimeno, grant title owner of Rancho Salsipuedes (meaning "get out if you can"). Within months of Hill's arrival, a potato boom was on and other settlers rushed to join in the successful venture. The budding town of Watsonville was one enormous potato field by 1853. GBK worked briefly on Hill's farm in 1851, in an effort to repay Horace Greeley for her passage West. Hill's home was on what was later known as the Silliman ranch, and in 1853, Jesse D. Carr planted there the first apple trees in the valley. Hill and his wife Eleanor and daughter Ella remained close friends of GBK until they moved southward late in 1853, after a glut on the potato market. SCE, p. 168.

12. The Buckle brothers, Thomas and William (also referred to in some sources as Bocle or Thompson) were from London. In 1838 William was granted the Rancho La Carbonera, which was located near the land that Eliza Farnham inherited.

13. John Cotter Pelton, a young New England schoolteacher and layman of the Baptist Church, came to California in 1849, to establish free public schools. He opened a school in San Francisco on December 26, 1849, in

the First Baptist Church and in March 1850, this school was adopted by the city and became the first public school in California. Mildred Brooke Hoover, *Historic Spots in California*, 3d ed., by Mildred Brooke Hoover, Hero Eugene Rensch, and Ethel Grace Rensch, rev. by William N. Abeloe (Stanford: Stanford University Press, 1966), pp. 354–355.

14. William Fitzpatrick, according to Helen Giffen's notes, died in Sacramento some years after the divorce.

15. "Paracelsus," a poem by Robert Browning, written in 1835, in which the hero, Paracelsus, declared as the ideal "To see good in evil, and a hope in ill-success."

16. Henry James, Sr. (1811–1882), clergyman, author, and lecturer, father of the novelist Henry James, rebelled against Calvinism and was strongly influenced by the mystical doctrines of Swedenborg.

17. William Ellery Channing (1780–1842) and Theodore Parker (1810–1860) were American Transcendentalists and Unitarian clergyman who GBK met at Brook Farm. Both were active in their opposition to slavery and war, and Parker, later, to the subjugation of women. The work of Thomas Carlyle (1795–1881), the Scottish essayist and historian, had a major impact on the American writers whom GBK knew and whose work she read and admired.

18. The *New York Tribune*, founded in 1841 by Horace Greeley, set a new standard in American journalism with contributors such as Charles Dana, George Ripley, and Margaret Fuller. The *National Anti-Slavery Standard* and the *Pennsylvania Freeman*, which was edited by John Greenleaf Whittier, were two major anti-slavery newspapers.

19. Henry Clay (1777–1852), John Calhoun (1782–1850), and Daniel Webster (1782–1852) were all more conservative statesmen than those GBK admired. Horace Mann (1796–1859), Charles Sumner (1811–1874), Joshua Giddings (1795–1846), Wendell Phillips (1811–1884), and William Lloyd Garrison (1805–1879) were prominent educators, statesmen, or abolitionists whose views GBK strongly supported.

20. GBK lived with the Purvis family in Byberry, Pennsylvania, for eighteen months. Robert Purvis, whose father was white and mother black, was an ardent abolitionist. George Bradford, who GBK knew from Brook Farm, was Sarah Bradford Ripley's brother. Sarah was Ralph

Waldo Emerson's aunt. It was at the home of Moses Atwood in Alton, Illinois, that GBK had boarded while teaching at the Monticello Female Academy.

21. When GBK lived in Pennsylvania, which she referred to as the "borderland of slavery," she often attended Quaker, anti-slavery meetings, where she heard Lucretia Mott speak.

22. Harriet Beecher Stowe's long tale of slavery, based on her reading of abolitionist literature and on her personal observations in Ohio and Kentucky, was published serially in the *National Era* in 1851–1852 and as the book *Uncle Tom's Cabin, or, Life Among the Lowly,* in 1852.

23. John Daubenbiss came to America from Bavaria in 1835. He moved to Soquel in 1845, where he and John Hames built a sawmill for Martina Castro. He was named road commissioner for Soquel in 1850 and in 1858 was elected supervisor.

24. Albert Brown later became foreman of the Davis & Jordan limestone quarry. In 1861 he was elected captain of the Santa Cruz contingent that responded to a call from Governor John Downey for organization of a regiment of infantry and five companies of cavalry for protection of the overland mail routes in support of the Union cause. After the company was mustered out in 1864, Captain Brown re-enlisted and remained a soldier until 1866. From 1870 to 1874 he served as Santa Cruz County Clerk, Auditor, and Recorder. He married Catherine Maria Hecox Tilden (called "Maria" in the journal) after the death of her first husband. He died April 12, 1919. SCE, p. 154. His brother was Wilmer Brown.

25. Henry George Atkinson and Harriet Martineau, *Letters on the Laws of Man's Nature and Development* (1851). Atkinson, a noted free-thinker, mesmerist, and phrenologist, co-authored the popular book with Martineau, the English novelist and political economist.

26. Paulina Kellogg Wright Davis (1813–1876), the active supporter of temperance, abolition, women's rights, and other reforms, was the organizer of the first National Woman's Rights Convention, over which she presided in Worcester, Massachusetts, in October 1850. In 1853 she established *Una,* one of the first women's rights periodicals, which she edited with Caroline Dall. *Famous American Women: A Biographical Dictionary from Colonial Times to the Present,* edited by Robert McHenry (New York: Dover Publications, 1980), p. 94. The Raritan Bay Union was

founded in 1853 near Perth Amboy, New Jersey. The colony, headed by Marcus Spring, was formed as a joint-stock company. The Grimké sisters, Sarah and Angelina Grimké Weld, taught at the colony's progressive school. Henry David Thoreau, Horace Greeley, and Bronson Alcott were lecturers there. The colony survived until 1856.

27. Prior to construction of wharves, cargo was either dragged through the surf and hoisted aboard schooners or carried on men's shoulders to smaller boats that conveyed them to ships. SCE, p. 130.

28. This following passage was selected for publication as Document 47 in *Victorian Women: A Documentary Account of Women's Lives in Nineteenth-Century England, France, and the United States* (Stanford: Stanford University Press, 1981, pp. 211–213), as an example of the theme of the lack of companionship experienced by women in the predominantly male world of the Far West.

29. Col. Whiting was married to Sue Colegrove, whose sister Olive Colegrove married Cornelius Cole in 1853. In 1853 the Coles visited Santa Cruz and may have been the guests GBK mentions in the journal entry of May 21. See also journal note 57. Cornelius Cole, *Memoirs* (New York: McLoughlin Bros., 1908), pp. 100, 102-103. David A. Dryden had been transferred from the Ohio Methodist Conference to California in 1851. His wife, Sarah Raynor Dryden, was the daughter of an English local preacher. She was intelligent, well educated, and a poet. Many of her poems were published in periodicals of the time. Dryden later authored a book denying the resurrection and fell into disfavor with the church. In 1875 he was employed by the government to look after the mission Indians in Southern California. He eventually joined the New Jerusalem Church. He died July 6, 1894. FYM, pp. 55–56, 64–65.

30. *Reveries of a Bachelor* is a series of essays which Donald Grant Mitchell published under the pseudonym of Ik Marvel in 1850.

31. William Tell Coleman (1824–1893) came to California in 1849 and became a successful merchant in the mining towns and in San Francisco. He was the leader of the San Francisco Vigilance Committees of 1851 and 1856.

32. Perhaps this is a reference to M. A. W. Johnson, rather than M. and W. Johnson. GBK had known Mary Anne White and Oliver Johnson for several years. GBK and Mary Anne served together as assistant matrons at

Sing Sing Prison. Mary Anne was not only a promoter of prison reform, but was also a lecturer on anatomy and physiology to women, an assistant to Horace Greeley on the *New York Tribune*, and an activist with her husband Oliver in the anti-slavery movement.

33. Sarah Shaw may be the Sarah B. Shaw whom GBK mentions in *Years of Experience*. Sarah Blake Sturgis Shaw was married to Francis George Shaw a philanthropist and literary translator who lived near Brook Farm. Their daughter Anna married George William Curtis, whom GBK knew at Brook Farm. Curtis was an author and editor of *Harper's Weekly*, where he often wrote for the enfranchisement of women and on other social reforms.

34. Oliver Johnson (1809–1889), anti-slavery leader and editor of the *National Anti-Slavery Standard.*

35. Lucretia Mott (1793–1880), American social reformer and Quaker minister. She was instrumental in calling the first women's rights convention at Seneca Falls, New York, in 1848. She was an ardent abolitionist.

36. *The History of Pendennis: His Fortunes and Misfortunes, His Friends, and His Greatest Enemy* is a work by the English novelist, William Makepeace Thackeray (1811–1863).

37. Ora was named for GBK's good friend, Deborah "Ora" Gannett Sedgwick. GBK first met Ora when Ora visited her uncle, the Reverend Ezra Gannett, in Boston, where GBK worked as a governess. Ora was also at Brook Farm and wrote of her experience in "A Girl of Sixteen at Brook Farm," *Atlantic Monthly*, 85 (March 1900): 394–404. Ora married C. B. Sedgwick, the brother of the author Catharine Maria Sedgwick.

38. Mrs. Frick was the wife of George W. Frick, the last teacher of the Methodist Academy, which preceded the public school. The Fricks went from Santa Cruz to Petaluma and then to Lompoc, where they both died. Mrs. Frick was the sister of J. W. Bryant, a member of the California Methodist Conference. It was the Frick's house and lot that the Kirbys bought when they moved into town in 1854. FYM, p. 79; SCE, p. 140.

39. Rancho Zayante (also spelled Sayanta, Sayante, or Siant).

40. Dr. John T. McLean had been an unsuccessful candidate for the

first state senate in 1849. SCE, p. 122.

41. *The Caxtons* is a novel by Bulwer-Lytton. Published in 1849, it tells the story of an upper middle-class English family. Thackeray's *Vanity Fair* was published in 1847–1848.

42. Justus Starr Redfield, the publisher of Edgar Allan Poe, had his headquarters in the same building with Fowler and Wells, the New York publishers.

43. The Kirby home was on a 1.2 acre parcel between Green and upper Union streets. (The ranch was sold in 1855.) The Kirby home on Mission Street originally stood on the south side, where Chestnut Street Extension is now. A new wing was later built onto the original structure, and in 1888 the old mid-section was moved to its present site at 117 Jordan Street. SWC, pp. 147–149. After Kirby closed his Glen Canyon tannery in 1855, he purchased another in partnership with Edmund Jones and Joseph Boston in the Escalona-Storey streets area. In 1863 he sold out to his partners and built another business on Laurel Street. This tannery was situated on both sides of Laurel, almost from Mission Street to the bottom of the hill. The tannery water wheel was powered by water from Majors Creek above. It operated until 1893. SCE, p. 140.

44. The Reverend Rufus Putnam Cutler of Portland, Maine, "a refined, scholarly man, quiet and reserved in habit," preached his first sermon to his San Francisco congregation on September 10, 1854. In November 1855, the Unitarian Church was incorporated in California. Although a Unitarian service was held in San Francisco as early as 1850, few Unitarian ministers were attracted to service in California. Cutler left San Francisco in 1859. It was not until 1866 that a Unitarian church was gathered in Santa Cruz by the Reverend Charles Gordon Ames. Arnold Crompton, *Unitarianism on the Pacific Coast: The First Sixty Years* (Boston: Beacon Press, 1957), pp. 17, 58–59.

45. Kate Imus, the daughter of Hiram Imus, Jr., married the blacksmith W. J. Hunter. The Hunters went south in the migration of a dozen Santa Cruz families in the seventies to the Cholame Valley in northern San Luis Obispo County. SWC, p. 95.

46. George Combe sought to popularize and institutionalize phrenology and to use it as a vehicle for social reform. His most significant work was *The Essay on the Constitution of Man*. Horace Mann was greatly

influenced by Combe's work and based many of his educational theories upon phrenology. John Davies, *Phrenology: Fad and Science; A 19th Century American Crusade* (New Haven: Yale University Press, 1955) pp. 85–86.

47.   Francois Guizot (1787–1874), the French statesman and historian. His monumental *General History of Civilization in Modern Europe* was translated into English by William Hazlitt in 1846.

48.   The Reverend John Sheridan Zelie arrived in Santa Cruz in 1851, the city's first Congregational minister.

49.   The Reverend Ezra Stiles Gannett, the Boston Unitarian clergyman who was GBK's first employer in America.

50.   William Ware (1797–1852), American author and clergyman, who is best known for his trilogy on the struggles of the early Christians— *Zenobia* (1837), *Aurelian* (1838), and *Julian* (1841). Sylvester Judd (1813–1853), Unitarian clergyman and author of *Margaret* (1845).

51.   Harriet Mead (1831–1920), moved to California in 1858 and married William Blackburn in 1859. Her sister Almira (1817–1885) married Dr. Francis M. Kittridge (1810–1879), who came to California in 1849 and to Santa Cruz in 1851. He was a graduate of Dartmouth Medical College and practiced medicine in Chelmsford and Lowell, Massachusetts, for twenty-six years before moving to Santa Cruz, where he never practiced but served as a consultant. W. D. and Kate Farrand are both buried in Evergreen Cemetery. Rowland states that Farrand and Judge Henry Rice, "southern-born and leading Democrats," presented a set of resolutions at a mass meeting held on May 8, 1861, which "condoned secession and attacked the coercion which the Washington government was assertedly using to keep the slave states in the federation. [These] resolutions were voted down overwhelmingly." SCE, p. 153. Rice's wife Lucy was the landlady of the Lorenzo Exchange Hotel. She was the aunt of Kate Imus . Lucy M. Rice died June 14, 1898.

52.   The slavery debate was an economic and political issue in the western territories. Immigration of blacks was permitted and slavery was outlawed when California became a state in 1850—although slave owners were allowed to reclaim fugitives up to 1858. Blacks who settled here were still vulnerable as long as they were forbidden to testify in court, and they did without this privilege until 1863. It was only after ratification of the

Fifteenth Amendment in 1870 that blacks could vote and serve as jurors.

It was therefore a bold move for Robert Johnson to insist on integrated education for his children. An illiterate black farmer from Tennessee, Johnson and his wife Sarah bought land in Watsonville in 1858 and immediately approached the school asking that the Johnson children be admitted. The family quickly became the center of a controversy in Watsonville that lasted a dozen years.

Ultimately, Johnson offered part of his own land "to be used for a school site for a school house to which children shall be admitted irrespective of color for the purposes of education...." Early in 1867, construction began on the "colored school" that now stands as a portion of the structure at 507 East Lake Avenue, Watsonville.

Ida May: A Story of Things Actual and Possible (1854), by Mary Langdon, and *Caste: A Story of Republican Equality* (1856), by Sydney A. Story, Jr., popular, melodramatic, anti-slavery novels, were both written under pseudonyms by Mary Hayden Green Pike (1824–1908). *Ida May* is the tale of a white child kidnapped into slavery and *Caste* is the story of a quadroon woman forbidden to marry a white man.

53. Mrs. Margaret Sinclair Voorhees was a friend of both GBK and Eliza Farnham. It was at her home in New York that EF died.

54. It was with Edmund Jones (d. 1903) and Joseph Boston as partners that Richard Kirby built his second tan yard. The firm was known as Kirby, Jones & Co. SCC, p. 26.

55. James A. Morgan (1838–1859) is buried in Evergreen Cemetery.

56. Martin C. Briggs, brother of H. W. Briggs, who served as a judge in Pacific Grove. FYM, pp. 33–35.

57. Catherine Maria Hecox (d. 1934) married first Dr. William Peregrine Tilden (d. 1873) and then Captain Albert Brown. Catherine and Dr. Tilden's son, Douglas (1860–1935), who lost his hearing and voice at an early age, became a noted sculptor. Dr. Tilden was elected to the state assembly and later became resident physician at the Stockton Insane Asylum. Cornelius Cole (1822–1924) practiced law in New York before coming to California in the gold rush. He continued his practice in Sacramento and published the city's *Times* with James McClatchey. He was an organizer of the Republican Party and a supporter of the Union. He served in the U.S. Congress (1863–1865) and the Senate (1867–1873). On March 15, 1859, a month-and-a-half after GBK wrote this entry, Margaret

Ellen Hecox died at the age of 15. She is buried in Evergreen Cemetery.

58. Mary Jane Morgan married William Rulofson in 1867.

59. Joseph W. Morgan died on October 20, 1863, at the age of 32 and is buried in Evergreen Cemetery. Salome Morgan married a Mr. Fridley. Rollo was a character created by Jacob Abbott for a series of instructive children's books first published in 1835 in Boston.

60. Epes Sargent (1813–1880), journalist, poet, dramatist, and advocate of spiritualism, published a series of standard school readers beginning in 1855. Tom Thumb is a traditional folk-tale character dating in print from the sixteenth century. The term "Tom Thumb" became the standard name for "little people" when P. T. Barnum presented the American, Charles Stratton (1838–1883), known as General Tom Thumb. Rather than Peter Spekter, GBK is probably referring to the fables of Otto Spekter (1807-1871), the German illustrator whose best known book was a collection of fables by Wilhelm Hey, translated by Mary Howitt. *The History of the Five Little Pigs,* is probably *The History of the Three Little Pigs,* a folk-tale collected by J. O. Halliwell in 1853.

61. Edward F. Porter, his brother Ben, and six cousins came to California in 1849 or soon after and most of them established themselves in Soquel in the spring of 1853. Ben Porter and his cousin, George K., established a tannery in Porter Gulch. According to Rowland, Dr. Asa W. Rawson had brought his wife and children from Illinois in 1853 to Santa Cruz, where he earned his living by operating the Union Livery Stable. Rawson died in 1868. He and his wife Harriet are buried in Evergreen Cemetery. William Anthony was a cousin of Elihu Anthony. In the later fifties Anthony erected a two-story wooden building for his hardware store and tin shop at the foot of Mission Hill. The Taylor referred to may have been Nelson Taylor, who was very active in the establishment of the Congregational Church in Santa Cruz.

62. William Anthony and Elizabeth Ruffner (Mrs. Joseph) were two of the original twelve members of the Congregational Church of Santa Cruz. *A Century of Christian Witness: History of First Congregational Church, Santa Cruz, California* (Santa Cruz: Sentinel Printers, 1963), p.158.

63. N. W. Slocum issued the first *Santa Cruz Weekly News* on August 17, 1859. The paper lasted until the following July, when Slocum moved the plant to San Jose, bought out F. B. Murdoch of the *Telegraph,* and

founded the *San Jose Mercury*. SCE, p. 207. The *Pacific Sentinel*, the rival newspaper, printed a brief obituary on the demise of the *News* on July 21, 1860: "Died of starvation at Santa Cruz, the Santa Cruz News, aged eleven months...though stuffed to repletion with unsubstantial pablum. Peace be to its ashes."

64. Perhaps Mrs. Sarah M. Clarke, who published the weekly *Contra Costa* in Oakland in 1855, and also authored a volume entitled *Teachings of the Age*. *The History of Woman Suffrage*, ed. Elizabeth Cady Stanton, Susan B. Anthony, Matilda Joslyn Gage, et al., 6 vols. (New York: Fowler & Wells, 1881–1886), III, p.761. Sarah M. Clarke and Eliza Farnham also were contributors to the *Hesperian*, a semi-monthly magazine for women which began publication in 1858 in San Francisco.

65. David C. Broderick (1820–1859) was born in Ireland and came to California in 1849. He became a U. S. Senator in 1859. He was violently opposed to the senior senator, William Gwin, a supporter of slavery who controlled federal patronage in the state. He denounced Gwin's champion, California Chief Justice David Terry, who challenged Broderick to a pistol duel. The duel took place near Lake Merced, where Terry mortally wounded Broderick, who was mourned as a martyr.

66. Catherine Sinclair (1817–1891), wife of the distinguished American actor, Edwin Forrest (1806–1872) and sister of Margaret Sinclair Voorhees, came to San Francisco to open the new Metropolitan Theater on Christmas Eve, 1853. She had divorced Forrest after ten years of marriage. Their sensational divorce trial had concluded in 1853, but the suit hung on for sixteen years. She was finally awarded $3,000 a year in alimony. In 1860 Catherine left the stage and retired to an estate on Staten Island, NY, where she lived with her sister Virginia (Mrs. Henry Sedley). *Notable American Women, 1607–1950* (Cambridge, Mass.: Harvard University Press, 1971), I, pp.646–647.

Genealogy

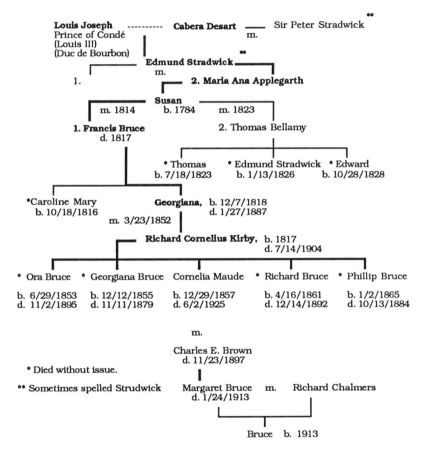

Louis Joseph ---------- **Cabera Desart** ———— Sir Peter Stradwick [**]
Prince of Condé   m.
(Louis III)
(Duc de Bourbon)

Edmund Stradwick [**]
m.

1.   **2. Maria Ana Applegarth**

Susan
m. 1814   b. 1784   m. 1823

1. Francis Bruce   2. Thomas Bellamy
d. 1817

* Thomas   * Edmund Stradwick   * Edward
b. 7/18/1823   b. 1/13/1826   b. 10/28/1828

*Caroline Mary   **Georgiana,** b. 12/7/1818
b. 10/18/1816   d. 1/27/1887
m. 3/23/1852

Richard Cornelius Kirby, b. 1817
d. 7/14/1904

* Ora Bruce   * Georgiana Bruce   Cornelia Maude   * Richard Bruce   * Phillip Bruce

b. 6/29/1853   b. 12/12/1855   b. 12/29/1857   b. 4/16/1861   b. 1/2/1865
d. 11/2/1895   d. 11/11/1879   d. 6/2/1925   d. 12/14/1892   d. 10/13/1884

m.

Charles E. Brown
d. 11/23/1897

* Died without issue.

** Sometimes spelled Strudwick   Margaret Bruce   m.   Richard Chalmers
d. 1/24/1913

Bruce   b. 1913

Ora Bruce Kirby died of consumption, at the age of forty-two, after an illness of a year. Prior to her illness, she had just completed arrangements for going to England to be married to a Mr. Watson, who is described in her obituary as a well known artist and Royal Academician. The obituary that appeared on the front page of the *Santa Cruz Sentinel* on November 5, 1895, was written by C. W. Doyle. Doyle described Ora as "one of the most notable women who ever lived in this city." Articles by Ora appeared frequently in the *Santa Cruz Surf*, including her observations on a trip she took to Japan in 1886. The author Caroline Dall, who visited the Kirby's in 1880, described Ora as her charming travelling companion. Mrs. Dall related Ora's description of her attempts to get a school in Virginia City and her teaching experiences in Carson. Caroline Dall, *My First Holiday* (Boston: Roberts Bros., 1881), p. 314.

The second daughter, Georgiana Bruce Kirby, died a month before her twenty-fourth birthday. Her obituary in the *Santa Cruz Sentinel* of November 22, 1879, describes her as a "a young lady of remarkable talent and individuality of character." She was educated at Swarthmore College, the Quaker college in Pennsylvania, and taught for two years in one of the public schools in Santa Cruz. "Her quiet firmness, sweetness of disposition, ripe culture combined with a genius for order and command, made her one of the most successful and popular teachers in the city." In her memory, the public school closed for one day.

Cornelia Maude Kirby, who Georgiana described in her journal as being "more delicate," with less power of resistance and endurance, outlived all of her siblings, dying in 1925 at the age of 68. Both her husband Charles E. Brown and her daughter, who married Richard Chalmers, died young, leaving Georgiana's sole surviving descendant, Bruce Chalmers.

Richard Bruce Kirby died in 1892 at the age of thirty-one in St. Louis. He had survived a mugging in Chicago, where he had lived for nearly ten years previous, working for the Hall Safe Company. Several months later he succumbed from complications due to the beating.

The youngest child, Phillip Bruce, died in 1884, at the age of nineteen. He was attending the Jesuit College of Santa Clara when Mrs. Dall visited in 1880. He was taken ill while at school at the University of California in Berkeley and died after a long and painful illness. His obituary in the October 14, 1884 *Santa Cruz Surf* called him "a lad of unusually bright promise." The *Santa Cruz Sentinel* obituary on the following day characterized him as "generous to a fault, a whole-souled and a true-friend." He was a member of the Class of '87 at the University and members of his class came to Santa Cruz to act as his pallbearers.

Bibliography

Books and Articles by Georgiana Bruce Kirby

"Before I Went to Brook Farm," *Old and New*, 3 (February 1871): 175-185.

"My First Visit to Brook Farm," *Overland Monthly*, 5 (July 1870): 9-19.

"Reminiscences of Brook Farm," *Old and New*, 3 (April 1871): 425-438.

"Reminiscences of Brook Farm," *Old and New*, 4 (September 1871): 347-358.

"Reminiscences of Brook Farm," *Old and New*, 5 (May 1872): 517-530.

"Tale of the Redwoods," *Overland Monthly*, 12 (1873): 212

Transmission: Or, Variation of Character Through the Mother. New York: S. R. Wells, 1877.

Years of Experience: An Autobiographical Narrative. New York: Putnams, 1887.

Letters

GBK to Sarah Edes Allen, Eyrie, Brook Farm, Saturday Night, [between Summer 1842 and April 1844].GBK was a friend of Sarah Allen and her brother, Daniel,when they were living in Boston. Sarah Allen later married John Lindsay Swift. Their son Lindsay Swift was the author of *Brook Farm: Its Members, Scholars, and Visitors* (New York: Macmillan, 1900), which is considered one of the best histories of Brook Farm that is available. The letter from GBK to Sarah Allen was first published in this work.

GBK to John Sullivan Dwight, Alton, Illinois, 18 January 1846. Dwight (1813–1893) was a member of Brook Farm and later a music editor. His journal, *Dwight's Journal of Music,* which was published for thirty years, was an important factor in the development of American musical taste. The letter is in the John Sullivan Dwight Collection of the Boston Public Library.

GBK to Charlotte Fowler Wells, Santa Cruz, 1851? Fowler and Wells was a famous New York firm of phrenologist-publishers, including the brothers Lorenzo Niles Fowler and Orson Squire Fowler, their sister Charlotte Fowler Wells, and her husband Samuel Roberts Wells. The letter is in the Fowler-Wells Collections, Collection of Regional History and University Archives, Cornell University. It was published in Madeleine B. Stern's, "Two Letters from the Sophisticates of Santa Cruz," *The Book Club of California Quarterly News-Letter,* 33(3) (Summer 1968): 51-62.

About the Contributors

Helen Giffen is an author and historical researcher who has worked in her profession nearly seventy years. A native of Alabama, she came to California with her family as an infant and became interested in the history of the West while still a young girl. She began to write at the age of ten and published her works, including poetry and fiction, for the first time in 1913-14, in the *Los Angeles Times*. She served as secretary to the Society of California Pioneers from 1942 to 1970, when she retired and moved to Los Gatos. She has written nine books with a California history theme, plus numerous articles for magazines and historical publications. Among her works are *The Life of Mariano Guadalupe Vallejo; Newspapers of the Mother Lode, 1850–1880; Historical Adobe Houses of California; Casas and Courtyards; The Diaries of Peter Decker; Overland to California, 1849; The Story of El Tejon; The Story of Golden Gate Park;* and her most recent, *Man of Destiny: The Life of Pierson Barton Reading, Pioneer of Shasta County, California,* published by the Shasta County Historical Society in 1985.

Carolyn Heebner Swift is a native of Watsonville, California and a third generation Santa Cruz County resident. She began collecting old photographs, interviewing pioneers, and writing historical articles as reporter for the *Watsonville Register-Pajaronian & Green Sheet.* She has long taken an active interest in women's issues, having served in 1973 as co-ordinator for the Santa Cruz County Chapter of the National Organization for Women (NOW). She has lectured on Georgiana Bruce Kirby and Eliza Farnham before many local organizations and history classes. She co-authored the work *Soquel Landing to Capitola-by-the Sea* with Cabrillo College professor Sandy Lydon in 1978 and continues to write on historical topics for regional publications. She resides in one of the earliest farmhouses (1878) built in Soquel, California.

Judith Steen is a reference librarian at the University of California, Santa Cruz. She holds degrees from the University of Washington and the University of Portland. She is a past president of the Santa Cruz Historical Society and a founding member of the Genealogical Society of Santa Cruz County and the Santa Cruz County Historical Trust. She is a member of the National Trust for Historic Preservation, the Victorian Society of America, and the California Historical Society. She lives in a house that was built the same year Georgiana began her diary and which is situated a half block from Georgiana and Richard Kirby's "droll little house" near the Mission Santa Cruz.

Madeleine B. Stern is a partner in the rare book firm of Leona Rostenberg and Madeleine B. Stern, New York. She is the author of numerous books and articles on 19th century Americana, feminism and publishing history, including, *The Life of Margaret Fuller; Louisa May Alcott; Purple Passage: The Life of Mrs. Frank Leslie; Heads and Headlines: The Phrenological Fowlers; Books and Book People in Nineteenth-Century America; Publishers for Mass Entertainment in Nineteenth-Century America; and A Phrenological Dictionary of Nineteenth-Century Americans.*

Index